ANGELS FROM THE SEA: RELIEF OPERATIONS IN BANGLADESH, 1991

U.S. Marines in Humanitarian Operations

by

Charles R. Smith

HISTORY AND MUSEUMS DIVISION
HEADQUARTERS, U.S. MARINE CORPS
WASHINGTON, D.C.

1995

For sale by the U.S. Government Printing Office
Superintendent of Documents, Mail Stop: SSOP, Washington, DC 20402-9328
ISBN 0-16-048458-8

Foreword

The first half of 1991 was a demanding time for the armed forces of the United States. In January, while elements of U.S. Army, Air Force, Navy, and Marines were still deploying to the Persian Gulf, where they would join other coalition forces in the liberation of Kuwait, a Marine special purpose force conducted Operation Eastern Exit, a daring rescue of American citizens and foreign nationals trapped in the American Embassy at Mogadishu, Somalia. Two weeks later Operation Desert Storm began and coalition aircraft flew against Iraqi targets in the Kuwaiti and Iraqi theaters of operation. In February, coalition ground forces slashed through the vaunted Saddam Line to liberate Kuwait, while their comrades afloat conducted one of the most successful strategic deceptions in military history. Soon thereafter, American and other coalition forces were involved in concurrent humanitarian operations, Provide Comfort in northern Iraq and Sea Angel in Bangladesh. In June, Mount Pinatubo in the Philippines erupted, causing massive damage. In response, American forces participated in Operation Fiery Vigil, the evacuation of Clark Air Force and Subic Bay Naval Bases, and Cubi Point Naval Air Station. With so much happening in so short a period, some of these operations did not receive the same amount of attention they would have, had they transpired during less tumultuous times. This monograph provides a detailed look at Joint Task Force Sea Angel, the first joint task force to be formed around a nucleus drawn from a Marine Air-Ground Task Force, and the Marine-led humanitarian relief effort in Bangladesh.

The end of the Cold War begat a revolution in American military strategy. Instead of a doomsday confrontation between superpowers, visionaries of the new world order foresaw an emphasis on low intensity conflicts in the third world and military "operations other than war." In addition, increasing emphasis would be placed on teamwork or "jointness" within the armed services, the formation of international coalitions not only for combined military operations, but also for humanitarian relief activities, and close cooperation among U.S. Government departments and agencies and international relief organizations. Operation Sea Angel validated the effectiveness of each. Sea Angel has served and can continue to serve as a model for future humanitarian operations in littoral areas.

The author of this volume Charles R. Smith, has been with the History and Museums Division since July 1971. He has written and edited several works on the early history of the Marine Corps, among them *Marines in the Revolution: A History of the Continental Marines in the American Revolution, 1775-1783* (Washington: Hist&MusDiv, HQMC, 1975). In addition, he is the author of *U.S. Marines in Vietnam: High Mobility and Standdown, 1969* (Washington: Hist&MusDiv, HQMC, 1988) in the official monographs of the Marine Corps in the Vietnam War, and the co-author of the forthcoming volume on U.S. Marine activities in Vietnam in 1968. He is a graduate of the University of California, Santa Barbara, and received his master's degree in history from San

Diego State University. He served in Vietnam with the 101st Airborne Division (Airmobile) in 1968 and 1969, first as an artilleryman and then as a historian.

In the pursuit of accuracy and objectivity, the History and Museums Division welcomes comments from interested individuals.

E. H. SIMMONS
Brigadier General
U.S. Marine Corps (Retired)
Director of Marine Corps History and Museums

Preface

Angels from the Sea: Relief Operations in Bangladesh, 1991, relies on primary source documents and oral history interviews for its main sources. Originals or copies of these records are held at the Marine Corps Historical Center. The documents include command chronologies, official messages, journal files, after action and special action reports, operation orders, and command briefs.

The author supplemented these sources with records provided by the other services, Department of State, Agency for International Development, international relief organizations, and pertinent published primary and secondary sources. Although none of the information in this history is classified, some of the documentation upon which it is based still carries a restricted or classified designation.

A number of reviewers, all of whom were participants in the events covered in the volume, read a comment edition of the manuscript. They were: Lieutenant General Henry C. Stackpole III, USMC (Ret); Ambassador William B. Milam; Dr. Mary C. Kilgour; Rear Admiral Stephen S. Clarey, USN (Ret); Brigadier General Peter J. Rowe, USMC (Ret); Brigadier General Randall L. West, USMC; Captain John R. Downs, MC, USNR; Colonel Gary W. Anderson, USMC; Colonel Stephen E. Lindblom, USMC (Ret); and Mr. Jon F. Danilowicz. Their comments, where applicable, have been incorporated into the text.

This history, like its subject, has been a cooperative effort. Lieutenant Colonel Ronald J. Brown, USMCR (Ret), former deputy command historian, then later, command historian, I Marine Expeditionary Force, aided the project by providing materials on the activities of the 5th Marine Expeditonary Brigade. Members of the Historical Branch, History and Museums Division, have reviewed the draft manuscript. Miss Evelyn A. Englander, head librarian, was very helpful in obtaining needed reference materials. Mr. Robert E. Struder, head of the Editing and Design Section, guided the manuscript through the various production phases. Mrs. Catherine A. Kerns contributed significantly to the publication effort, completing the design and layout, and Mr. William S. Hill, the division's visual information specialist, expertly produced the maps and assisted with the photo illustrations to the volume.

The author gives special thanks to Brigadier General Edwin H. Simmons, USMC (Ret), Director of Marine Corps History and Museums, whose policies guided the preparation of this history; to former Deputy Director, Marine Corps History and Museums, Colonel William J. Davis, USMC (Ret), who provided support and guidance; to Mr. Benis M. Frank, Chief Historian, who aided the author by giving him the benefit of his considerable experience in writing Marine Corps history; and to Dr. Jack Shulimson, Head, History Writing Unit, for providing advice and for editing the draft manuscript.

The author also is indebted to those individuals within the Marine Corps,

Department of Defense, and other U.S. Government departments and agencies who freely exchanged information and made pertinent documents and photographs available for examination. Among them were: Colonel Eugene L. Gobeli, USMC; Colonel Kevin M. Kennedy, USMC (Ret); Lieutenant Colonel Steven A. Slade, USA; Lieutenant Colonel Larry A. Johnson, USMC; Major V. M. Bentinck, RM; Dr. Richard W. Stewart; Captain Len Palaschak, USA; Chief Warrant Officer Larson P. Wilkison, USMC; Mr. Robert B. Hilton; and Mr. Dennis J. King. To these individuals and all others connected with this project, the author is indebted and truly grateful. In the end, however, it is the author alone who is responsible for the content of the text, including all opinions expressed and any errors of fact.

Charles R. Smith

Table of Contents

NOAA-11
Thermal
infrared
4/29/91
12:30 P.M.
Dacca time

BHUTAN

INDIA

BANGLADESH

*Dacca

NOAA

Angels from the Sea: Relief Operations in Bangladesh, 1991

The Winds of Death

On night of 29 April 1991 howling winds of death roared up the Bay of Bengal, signaling the arrival of a killer cyclone. For eight hours the densely populated coastal lowlands and offshore islands of the nation of Bangladesh on the Indian subcontinent were battered by 235 kilometer-per-hour (140-mile) gale-force winds and swamped by a six- to eight-meter tidal wave. The first rays of sunshine the next morning revealed almost unimaginable devastation. The entire southeast countryside was under water. Trees had been uprooted or stripped of their leaves and villages had been leveled. What had been a lush, verdant landscape was now muddy brown. The bodies of an estimated 139,000 people and more than a million livestock floated in turbid water. The affected area was completely isolated. There was no electricity, every phone line was down, and roads had been washed away. There was no way accurately to assess, let alone repair, the damage. A greater danger, however, was that the situation could get worse before it got better. Famine and disease threatened Bangladesh and without immediate action this fast-unfolding tragedy could become a humanitarian disaster of monumental proportions. The disaster would be averted as the Bangladesh government, with the assistance of a Marine-led, American military joint task force, turned back the threat.

The People's Republic of Bangladesh, formerly the east wing of Pakistan, is the world's most densely populated agrarian nation. This troubled land is no stranger to natural disasters. Located between India and Burma on the stunningly beautiful, fertile, deltaic plain formed by the confluence of three Asian river systems, the Brahmaputra, Ganges, and Meghna, Bangladesh is situated at the head of a natural funnel formed by the shallow Bay of Bengal. Ravaged by floods and tornadoes, the country has been subjected to seven of this century's deadliest cyclones. Between 1960 and 1971 alone, five cyclones killed more than 540,000 people. As one American newspaper reported: "These are seminal disasters, interspersed among scores of other ghastly events that seem almost minor by comparison--300 die in a train fire, 400 perish when a ferry boat goes under," or Bengal tigers kill 50 people in a forest along the coast.[1] During the annual monsoon season, from May to October, it is not unusual for the welcome floods which are the lifeblood of this country to exceed the norm and cause extensive crop loss and cholera, and gastrointestinal epidemics.

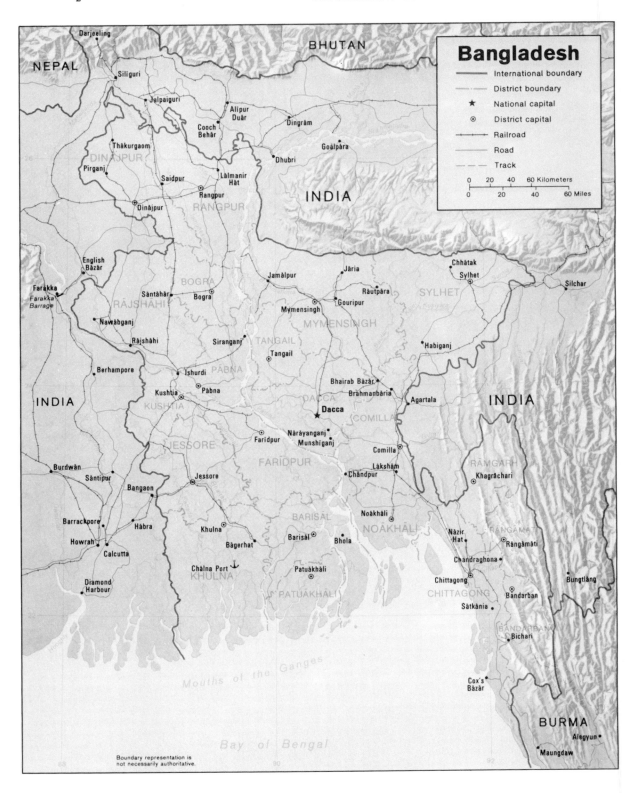

While the hurricanes of the Atlantic and Eastern Pacific and the typhoons in the Western Pacific are frequently more intense, the cyclones spawned in the Bay of Bengal often cause catastrophic loss of life and property due to Bangladesh's topography and population density. Since most of the country lies less than nine meters above sea level, a high tidal wave can sweep over most of the low-lying islands and immediate coastal areas. People, buildings, and crops surviving the initial onslaught are therefore at great risk of death and further damage until the waters recede, a process which can take weeks.

With about 116 million people occupying a nation the size of Wisconsin, overpopulation has forced large numbers of Bangladeshi to inhabit remote islands, silt islands or *chars*, and the coastal floodplain. The areas most vulnerable to the severe effects of cyclones are occupied by the poor and landless. They settle in the islands and coastal regions where they eke out a living without paying rent or sharecrop on land perennially at risk of inundation by salt water. Thus, it is the poor and landless who most often lose what little they have built and accumulated, and even a few days without food or income following a cyclone is a devastating experience from which they may never recover.

On 23 April 1991, the Bangladesh Space Research and Remote Sensing Organization detected a tropical depression just beyond the southern edge of the Bay of Bengal. As it moved northwest over the warm waters of the bay, the depression slowly evolved into a tropical storm and eventually became a cyclone. Meteorologists designated it Tropical Cyclone 02B.[2]

As early as the 24th, the Government of Bangladesh and international relief agencies issued storm warnings to alert the country's citizens, especially those living on off-shore islands and in coastal districts, of potential danger. Authorities urged the inhabitants of these vulnerable regions to move their families, domestic animals, and belongings into the relative safety of cyclone shelters, higher ground, or to areas at least 10 kilometers inland. The warning cautioned the people to bury food, drinking water, and medicine in sealed packets and cans. The containers, buried at least one meter underground, could be retrieved after the expected tidal surge had receded.[3]

As Tropical Cyclone 02B, now named Marian, moved slowly up the Bay of Bengal, thousands took refuge in cyclone shelters. Due to the lack of shelter space thousands more had to remain outside, seeking safety atop multistoried buildings and even in tall trees. Many people, however, stayed in their homes. They were skeptical of the warnings and weather forecasts, because for every actual cyclone there had been countless warnings. The fact that Marian had formed in the premonsoon season led many to believe that as previous early cyclones had it would pass by harmlessly. Others refused to leave their homes and the land they cultivated, fearing that since they possessed no title to the land they occupied, they could lose everything if someone else moved in while they were away. The government appeared to make little effort to evacuate those on vulnerable offshore islands.[4]

Photograph courtesy of Mary C. Kilgour

The barograph on board the Bangladeshi naval ship Umar Farooq, *which rode out the storm in the port of Chittagong. At 0145 on 30 April the drop in barometric pressure to below 930 millibars could no longer be recorded by the ship's instruments.*

On the 28th, Cyclone Marian assumed a more northeasterly direction. The Bangladesh government then activated its alert system, warning coastal and island residents of imminent danger from hurricane-force winds and the threat of a storm surge. Heavy winds and torrential rains began to buffet the country's southeast coast the following day. More than 320,000 Bangladeshi sought the protection of cyclone shelters and official buildings. The storm's death-blow came about midnight. Marian's center crossed the coast near the Meghna Estuary, located between the country's second largest city, Chittagong, and North and South Hatia Islands. A six- to eight-meter high tidal wave rolled over the low-lying off-shore islands, swept across the tidal plain, and then moved several kilometers inland. Plunged into darkness, the fortunate who had taken refuge in shelters watched in horror as their simply built homes, cattle, neighbors, and crops were swept away. Even substantial buildings trembled as if shaken by an earthquake before being hit by the tidal surge. "There was," as one observer noted, "an uncanny roaring sound of the whirlwind and on-rushing water grasping people and domestic animals into the jaws of death."[5]

On the morning of 30 April, all that was known in Dhaka, the capital, was that a cyclone causing uncertain damage had hit the islands and southeastern coastal areas. Telephone, FAX, and telegraph with the affected areas, as well as international communications, were down. While precise, verifiable

Photograph courtesy of Shahidul Alam

Cattle corpses lay in fields inundated by salt water on Sandwip Island. An estimated one million head of cattle perished during the storm.

information was unavailable, initial reports from the media, the government, and several voluntary agencies indicated that there was an unknown number of deaths and widespread property damage.[6]

Later that day, Prime Minister Begum Khaleda Zia flew to the affected areas and upon her return to Dhaka that evening called her cabinet into session.[*] Following the cabinet meeting, she issued an appeal for international assistance, noting that while it would take some time before the full "extent of the damage [is] clearly known and the requirement of the affected people fully realized, it is, however, evident that the damage has been both colossal and extensive." The government, she continued, "has mobilized all its manpower and resources, and already launched a massive relief operation, but the magnitude of the damage appears to be such that it might prove impossible for the government of Bangladesh alone to meet the challenge and mitigate the sufferings of the helpless

---

[*] Begum Khaleda Zia was the widow of former army general and President, Ziaur Rahman (Zia), who was assassinated by dissident elements of the military while visiting Chittagong in 1981. The killing of Zia was followed by nearly 10 years of rule by another general who became President, Hussain Muhammad Ershad. Ershad was forced to resign in December 1990 following a period of strikes, protests, and a general disintegration of law and order. In February 1991, an interim government oversaw new elections. As the country's new and first woman prime minister, Begum Khaleda Zia promised to restore parliamentary democracy to Bangladesh after taking power in March, just six weeks before the cyclone.

people." It was under these circumstances that she appealed to the international community "to come forward in aid of the humanity in distress in Bangladesh and help the people affected by the cyclone." Food, shelter, pure drinking water, medicine, and clothing were of immediate need.[7]

The government, which less than five months before had ended more than 15 years of military dictatorship, was unprepared to respond quickly and effectively to a disaster of this magnitude. Within days instead of hours, the young democratic government activated coordinating committees and mobilized its armed forces to restore access to clean drinking water, reestablish communications, and distribute relief supplies from its own stockpiles. Although the effort eventually would involve all elements of Bangladesh society, the armed forces were the key players initially. Constantly prepared for disaster operations, they could mobilize trained human resources with an effective chain of command, and operate on a decentralized basis when communications were inevitably knocked out. The army soon established temporary camps and began feeding refugees, while the Bangladesh air force, using the remaining dozen undamaged helicopters, began food and medicine drops to isolated communities.[8]

The international community responded more quickly. Neighboring India immediately sent aid supplies and three helicopters. Saudi Arabia, Canada, and the United Kingdom each pledged millions of dollars. China and Japan promised humanitarian aid. The European Economic Community undertook to send food, tents, clothing, medicine, and other essentials. Private relief agencies and non-government organizations, such as the Red Crescent Society, International Red Cross, Cooperative for American Relief Everywhere (CARE), World Health Organization, Oxford Committee for Famine Relief (OXFAM), and Caritas Bangladesh, activated volunteers and supplies already in Bangladesh and agreed to provide additional assistance.

In Dhaka, United States Ambassador William B. Milam, a career diplomat and an expert on international economic, environmental, and energy issues, rapidly moved to coordinate the American response. After receiving unconfirmed reports of widespread devastation on the 30th, he, at the request of the United States Agency for International Development (USAID) Mission Director Mary C. Kilgour, a former Marine Corps officer candidate with more than 25 years of service with the agency, declared a disaster and authorized the immediate release of $25,000 to the Bangladesh government for relief activities. In addition, an estimated $2 million worth of just-arrived medical supplies previously donated through the Department of Defense's Humanitarian Assistance Program, but not delivered, were turned over to the Ministry of Health. The 5,500 pounds of medical supplies included prepackaged kits containing surgical and first-aid equipment and intravenous fluids, which the Government of Bangladesh had requested the previous year. The American mission also took steps to obtain a comprehensive assessment of the situation by dispatching trained staff members from four USAID-funded non-government organizations to the affected areas with a standardized rapid assessment program developed by the mission.[9]

The following day, at the invitation of the Bangladesh government, Ambassador Milam and other heads of foreign missions toured the most devastated areas. In their discussions with local officials, they were told that the critical need was pure drinking water. "The tidal surge, river flooding and heavy rainfall," the embassy reported, "caused considerable damage to water distribution systems in built-up areas and flooded many of the shallow and deep 'tube wells' that the majority of the rural citizens use for fresh water." This lack of pure drinking water "will result in possible loss of life due to dysentery and other water related diseases."[10]

The mission's initial assessment was confirmed on 2 May. Prime Minister Zia, after meeting with representatives of non-government relief agencies, issued a fresh international appeal. She asked for an immediate $56 million in assistance, noting that the "threat to the cyclone survivors was from death due to dehydration, starvation and disease."[11] The government also requested the donation of a number of items which could be procured locally such as food and medicine, and items such as helicopters, tents, water purification tablets, and bleaching powder which were in short supply or could not be obtained in Bangladesh. These items were needed to supplement the government's on-going, yet uncoordinated, relief efforts.[12]

As a result of Prime Minister Zia's appeal and Ambassador Milam's visit, the mission, which saw the "supply of first and foremost fresh water and, secondly, potable water" as the greatest need, immediately donated more than 727,000 water purification tablets to the Bangladesh government and non-government organizations for distribution. Its supply depleted, the mission then sent an urgent request for funds to the Department of State's Office of Foreign Disaster Assistance (OFDA) to purchase additional purification agents and oral rehydration salts. The embassy also queried the Department of Defense (DOD) concerning the possibility of obtaining 2 million chlorine-based tablets from DOD stocks.* "We realize that the number is large," noted the defense attache, Lieutenant Colonel James A. Dunn, Jr., USA, "and that Operation Provide Comfort may have drawn down stocks." But, as he pointed out, "there are as many as one million plus families who will need fresh water each day until normal systems are restored."[13]**

With the deployment of an ever-increasing number of Bangladesh military personnel and non-government relief workers to the affected areas, the extent of the devastation gradually emerged. Ten districts, home to approximately 11.2

---

* Chlorine-based water purification tablets were preferred over the standard military canteen-type, iodine-based tablets as the latter posed problems if taken by pregnant women.

** A graduate of the Armed Forces Staff College and an Army tank officer, Lieutenant Colonel James A. Dunn attended the Bangladesh Staff College before being assigned as defense attache in 1989.

Photograph courtesy of USCinCPac

Housing was destroyed in Khankanabad, Banskhali, south of Chittagong.

Photograph courtesy of Shahidul Alam

This devastated patch on Sandwip Island was once home to 26 families.

million people, were affected by the cyclone. Of those ten, the four coastal districts of Bhola, Noakhali, Chittagong, and Cox's Bazar bore the brunt of the storm and storm surge. Within the four coastal districts the greatest concern was for the 5.2 million people living in 13 *upazilas* or administrative subdistricts, and the city of Chittagong, the historic city that served as a primary entry point for supplies destined for the China-Burma-India theater during World War II. By 2 May, the government confirmed more than 37,000 dead and reported tens of thousands missing. The death toll was expected to exceed 100,000, since the off-shore islands of Kutubdia, Sandwip, and Maheshkali, with a population of more than 600,000, virtually were submerged. Chittagong, the only port in the storm-ravaged region capable of receiving relief supplies, was blocked by sunken ships and its air facilities severely damaged.

Tragic stories equalled the number of bodies that washed ashore with the tide. One such was that of a desperate man in the village of Kutubdia who "reaches out for a floating banana tree on which to rest his baby boy. But a poisonous snake bites the man's arm and he drops silently into the turbid floodwaters. The tree floats away. The baby drowns." In the same village "another man blacked out at the sight of waves 'as high as mountains'. Hours later, when he came to, he realized that his wife, son and three daughters had been swept out to sea . . . . 'I have lost everything. I have lost everything,' the man said. 'God, why has it happened to me?'"[14] For those who survived the cyclone, they had to contend with cholera, shortages of food and water, and everyday bouts with malnutrition, dysentery, diarrhea, and malaria.

The American Relief Effort

On 3 May, President George Bush sent a message to Prime Minister Zia expressing his condolences and those of the American people over the devastation caused by the cyclone. "Our hearts go out . . . to the families of the numerous victims of this terrible tragedy," Presidential spokesman Marlin Fitzwater said. The United States stands ready, the President assured the Bangladesh government, to assist in the varied tasks of relief and reconstruction. In addition to the more than $2 million already provided, the United States, Fitzwater reported, was "looking into other means to help Bangladesh obtain its highest priority needs for clean water, dry food, helicopter transport, clothing, and temporary shelter."[15]

In Bangladesh, on the 3d, Agency for International Development Director Mary Kilgour, accompanied by Defense Attache Lieutenant Colonel James Dunn and First Lieutenant David Silverman, commanding officer of the U. S. Army's 2d Platoon, Company B, 84th Engineer Battalion (Combat) (Heavy), flew to

Photograph courtesy of Mary C. Kilgour

USAID Director Mary C. Kilgour hands over water purification tablets to Oli Ahmed, Civilian Relief Coordinator, at the Chittagong Circuit House Civilian Relief Center.

Chittagong to view the damage to the city and port.* The USAID director met with the Minister of Communications, Oli Ahmed, a native of Chittagong, who was coordinating the relief effort, and turned over 450,000 water purification tablets. Lieutenant Colonel Dunn and Lieutenant Silverman toured the heavily damaged port facilities and airfield with senior Bangladeshi military officials. Lieutenant Silverman determined that the repair of the airfield's terminal and tower was within the engineer detachment's capabilities. The following day Director Kilgour returned to Dhaka and Lieutenant Colonel Dunn flew to the offshore islands where he viewed the devastation.[16]

The four USAID-funded, non-government assessment teams made their first report, based on field trips to the affected areas, to the mission's staff on the 4th, the proclaimed national day of mourning for the flood victims. By then the country's confirmed death toll stood at 92,000, but the teams estimated that it would soon exceed 150,000. The total population in the moderate to severely affected areas they estimated at 5 million, half of whom were homeless. The off-

---

* When the cyclone struck, the 15 soldiers from 2d Platoon, Company B, were deployed to Mymensingh, north of Dhaka, constructing schools on training Exercise Baker Carriage II. The Pacific Command authorized the American Embassy to coordinate all United States military disaster assistance, including the diversion of the platoon from school construction to the relief effort. (USCinCPac msg to AmEmbassy, Dhaka, 010045ZMay91)

shore islands had no source of fresh water and it was unlikely that a fresh water supply would be reestablished for at least several weeks. The survivors, they reported, lacked water, food, shelter and had lost all of their possessions; the dead lacked adequate burial.

Of those inhabiting the rural coastal areas, 70 to 80 percent were homeless and more than a third of these were in overcrowded, dirty, unorganized shelters without sanitation or water supply. Many had not eaten in the last 24 to 48 hours. The teams noted that half the cattle and most of the fowl were lost. The dry season or *boro* rice crop was lost and they surmised that it could not be replanted for six months due to the inundation of salt water. In urban areas, such as Chittagong and Cox's Bazar, the poor suffered a near total loss of shelter, food supplies, fuel, and cooking utensils. The middle and upper classes lost less and had access to some food, however, with dry, unspoiled food in short supply, the teams reported that its price was beginning to climb sharply.[17]

The cyclone also ruined the affected area's infrastructure; by this time the reported damage was far worse than that inflicted by past cyclones. The large, just-completed bridge spanning the Karnaphuli River in Chittagong had been knocked down by an errant crane, making communications with the south more difficult. Hundreds of kilometers of embankments, used for flood protection and to prevent the inundation of crop lands by salt water, had been breached or tally destroyed by the storm surge. Major thoroughfares and sections of the Dhaka

Department of Defense Photo (USAF) DF-ST-92-02643

Salt water inundated the rice fields of Sandwip Island destroying much of the boro, *or dry season rice crop.*

Photograph courtesy of Shahidul Alam

People of Chowkatalli on Sandwip Island collect water from a tubewell just meters away from a pond containing both human and cattle remains.

to Chittagong railway were cut, as were telecommunications between the area and the capital. The area's only ground satellite station at Betbunia, northeast of Chittagong, was wrecked. It was estimated that it would take several weeks before satellite communications could be restored.[18]*

Access to fresh water, the non-government teams reported, should remain the first priority. If fresh water could not be procured, then water purification materials, such as tablets, or locally purchased alum or bleaching powder, needed to be distributed, followed by oral rehydration salts, and dry food which children could consume. The import and distribution of other items such as milk powder had to be discouraged. To assist with the distribution effort, the teams echoed the mission's conclusions and the request made by the Bangladesh government that the United States and several other bilateral donors provide flatbottomed, inflatable boats; helicopters; water containers; rations; and communications equipment.[19]

The mission relayed a brief outline of the teams' assessments, recommendations, and requests to the Department of State, which had established a working group on the American government's relief effort. In addition to the Department of State, the group was made up of representatives from AID's Office of Foreign Disaster Assistance, other units within AID, the Office of the

---

* Because international telephone and FAX were down, all communications between the embassy and Washington had to be by cumbersome cable.

Secretary of Defense, and appropriate sections of the Joint Staff. During the group's first meeting, its members determined that assuring an adequate supply of oral rehydration salts and water purification tablets was the highest immediate priority, and the item which the Office of Foreign Disaster Assistance would focus on even though its funding authority virtually was exhausted.

The problems of aid organization and distribution, however, dominated the working group's discussions. While the supply of food stockpiled in government warehouses, or "Go Downs," and non-government storehouses was considered adequate to deal with the disaster, the means of delivering the food to those in need was not. Department of Defense representatives, noting that they were still gathering information on the availability and exact cost of providing helicopters, most probably from the Philippines, estimated that it would cost in excess of $3 million to transport eight helicopters to Dhaka and that it would take a minimum of five days. With cost in mind, the group agreed that it might be more practical to charter helicopters or provide funds for helicopters from a third country, and that the money saved then be used for water and land transportation. Before any specific action could be taken, the group, in addition to passing on its thoughts, asked that the embassy provide "well-defined action recommendations both for immediate relief and for near-term reconstruction and rehabilitation efforts."[20]

While members of the working group continued their efforts in Washington, American Embassy personnel moved ahead in Dhaka. Agency for International Development representatives met with officials of the Bangladesh government and non-government relief agencies daily, constantly updating their assessment of the damage and need for assistance. They also began to make cash grants to several prequalified, non-government organizations to address immediate health needs, and requested an Office of Foreign Disaster Assistance allotment of an additional $4.25 million in grant funds to support the proposed relief efforts of other non-government organizations.[21] On the military side, Defense Attache Lieutenant Colonel Dunn queried Admiral Charles R. Larson, USN, United States Commander in Chief, Pacific (USCinCPac) on the availability of water containers and rations, and on the possibility of using satellite coverage for damage assessment. Informed by the Department of State and USAID that helicopters might have to be rented if needed, he also sent messages to nearby defense attaches inquiring if helicopters could be obtained and their rental rates.[22]

By 6 May, the confirmed death toll had risen to more than 125,000. The Bangladesh government reported that 77,800 confirmed dead were from Chittagong District, 39,700 from Cox's Bazar, and smaller numbers from the remaining hard-hit districts. Within Chittagong District, 35,000 of the dead were residents of Sandwip Island, more than 10 percent of the island's precyclone population; 30,000 from the subdistrict of Banshkhali, 10,000 from Anwara subdistrict; and 1,900 from the city itself. Even greater damage had occurred in the areas surrounding Cox's Bazar, where as much as 25 percent of the population of Kutubdia Island was reported killed. Women and children constituted more than 60 percent of all dead. The estimated number of homeless was placed between two and one half and three million people.

Photograph courtesy of Shahidul Alam

An urban bustee *or village in Chittagong, totally destroyed by the cyclone, was rebuilt temporarily on a roadside with salvaged bamboo and matting.*

That day, despite strong rains and heavy seas which had thwarted earlier attempts, several ships of the Bangladesh navy reached the offshore islands of Sandwip, Manpura, and Kutubdia, and began the task of setting up relief camps. Although hampering to the relief effort, the rains did provide the only fresh water the islanders, most of whom were marooned and hungry, had received since the cyclone struck a week before. As had the navy, the Bangladesh army deployed additional communications teams and troops to the affected areas to reestablish communications and assist with the daily airlift of more the 30 metric tons of bread. The government also sent additional companies of the Bangladesh Rifles, one of the country's two paramilitary forces, to assist local officials in maintaining order.[23] The efforts of the government, both civilian and military, were, as the American Embassy pointed out, heroic and involved numerous personal sacrifices, but the task was overwhelming.[24]

A week after the cyclone struck, relief workers had made little headway in reaching and aiding those in the greatest need of help. Dependent upon a few ships, a dozen of their own helicopters and three sent from India, the government's efforts moved ahead slowly. Although relief supplies poured in from around the world, the lack of adequate transportation hindered timely distribution of much-needed relief supplies. This prompted Ambassador Milam to request that Lieutenant Colonel Dunn ask CinCPac "if U.S. Marine Corps or U.S. Navy assets that may be transiting the Indian Ocean, southern Bay of Bengal or near Singapore might be diverted to assist in relief operations." Most important assets would include helicopters for the delivery of relief supplies and personnel and landing craft which would be able to reach nearby offshore islands. It was vital to land relief supplies, especially potable water, immediately. Lieutenant Colonel Dunn envisioned "that the ships could anchor off Chittagong for coordination with local government/military relief operators and then conduct operations under their control." While it was not clear at that time how long relief operations would continue, the Ambassador, Dunn noted, believed that the Navy or Marine Corps assets would be needed for at least two to three weeks. Should that long a stay prove a problem, their help for less time, he said, would still be extremely useful. Dunn also inquired whether units then deployed to Thailand on the Cobra Gold series of training exercises might be diverted to Bangladesh.[25]

In a separate request, Lieutenant Colonel Dunn reported that Ambassador Milam had been approached by Bangladesh officials and asked if the United States could assist by providing long-range communications and a "mini-air traffic control" unit to restore control of airspace in the disaster area. This was crucial because Bangladesh, Indian, and Pakistani helicopters were operating with no air traffic control.[26] Lieutenant Colonel Dunn also requested the use of a small, twin-engine Beechcraft support aircraft, to assist the staff of the embassy and defense attache's office in damage assessment.[27]

The use of American military aircraft, ships, and communications teams was being considered in Washington. In discussing the range of options available to assist the Bangladesh government's relief efforts, Defense Department representatives assigned to the Department of State working group reported that the nearest embarked helicopter assets, those of the 5th Marine Expeditionary Brigade (MEB), were in the Persian Gulf, but could not be diverted to Bangladesh as they were earmarked to support a possible evacuation of American

Photograph courtesy of Shahidul Alam
Hundreds of people line up near one of the first temporary emergency relief centers established by the Bangladesh government on Sandwip Island.

citizens from Ethiopia. The 5th MEB's redeployment also was tied to the safe withdrawal of U.S. Army forces from southern Iraq, the termination of Navy combat air patrols, and the movement of more than 30,000 Iraqi refugees to havens in Kuwait and Saudi Arabia.[28] The only other helicopter support options were to deploy a number of Marine Boeing CH-46 Sea Knight and Sikorsky CH-53 Sea Stallion helicopters attached to Contingency Marine Air-Ground Task Force 4-90 from the Philippines using Air Force Lockheed C-5A Galaxy transports or to airlift helicopters from Okinawa or the West Coast. Expenditures to support the latter options, defense representatives noted, would be prohibitive. The cost of each one-way C-5A sortie would approach $400,000, excluding fuel, maintenance, and associated charges. As to other forms of disaster assistance, such as food, water purification tablets, flatbottomed, inflatable or shallow-draft aluminum or fiberglass-hulled boats, and plastic water containers, the defense staffers reported the items could be procured if the Department of State provided the funds. The bottom line was that unless the President said "do it," or the Department of State found funds to pay the bill, there was little the Department of Defense could do.

The State Department informed the American Embassy in Dhaka of the problems and exorbitant costs of leasing commercial heavy-lift helicopters or transporting Department of Defense air assets. As the department noted: "we have conflicting information on the need for helicopters and need to sort out the requirements before we make a final decision on whether to proceed." The department also reported funding then under consideration would not authorize the use of commercial or Department of Defense helicopters. It concluded by asking the embassy to confirm its requirement for heavy-lift helicopters in view of the fact that the then-current level of funding did not include funds for helicopters: "We need urgently therefore your best needs assessment so that we can determine whether we should go ahead with our search for sources of funding."[29]

In reply to the department's request, Ambassador Milam noted that the "mission understands that OFDA and perhaps others think a substantial sum for helicopters could be better spent chartering or hiring boats. Initially [the] mission also [was] inclined toward that view." But, he continued, "we have lately become convinced . . . that U.S.-provided helicopters are essential to [the] relief efforts." In support of his position, Ambassador Milam noted that the most devastated areas where people were starving could only be reached by helicopter. Although the Government of Bangladesh possessed nearly 300 shallow-draft boats, donated by Japan in 1988, they could not, he reported, navigate open ocean in order to supply or resupply the hard-hit, offshore islands. Peripheral to the issue of disaster relief, but of extreme political importance, was that the Bangladesh government's first relief request made of the United States was for helicopters. A number of government officials, he noted, had speculated that the reason Bangladesh had not been supplied with helicopters was that the United States had no confidence in the "newly and fairly elected government." "While our calculations about the need for helicopters is not based on this factor," he

A local ferry sits abandoned in the midst of rice fields covered with salt water. Devastated areas such as this could only be reached by helicopter.

continued, "it is important that we be visibly responsive to this democratic government's urgently expressed needs." "If cost effectiveness and numbers of tons per blade hours is to be the guide for deciding whether helicopters should be sent to Bangladesh, then perhaps they should not be sent. If filling a desperate need, as stated by the BDG [Bangladesh government] and delivering food/supplies that will save lives is the primary consideration, then helicopters should be sent." Ambassador Milam strongly urged that $2 million be found to fund three heavy lift, Department of Defense CH-46 helicopters for a period of two weeks. Military aircraft, he concluded, would be administratively easier to support than commercially leased aircraft.[30]

While the Department of State tried to resolve diplomatic and financial difficulties, events in Ethiopia made U.S. military assistance to Bangladesh much more likely. At that time, the 5th MEB was embarked on board the ships of Amphibious Group 3 (PhibGru 3) in the Persian Gulf. This force had not been previously available because it was standing by to evacuate more than 600 American citizens caught up in a civil war in Ethiopia. In early May, even though rebel factions had gained ground against government forces, the threat subsided and the 5th MEB was no longer needed.

The 5th MEB and PhibGru 3 were reorganized in preparation for their redeployment in the wake of Operation Desert Storm and lost about one-third of their combat capability. The 11th Marine Expeditionary Unit (Special Operations Capable) (MEU [SOC]) and five amphibious ships of Amphibious Squadron 1 were detached from the 5th MEB and PhibGru 3, respectively. They were to stay in the Persian Gulf as a strategic reserve, covering Central Command's pull-out and ready to provide air and ground forces should an Ethiopian evacuation become necessary.* Two Military Sealift Command ships assigned to PhibGru 3, the crane ship *Flickertail State* (T-ACS 5) and the cargo ship *Cape Girardeau* (T-AK 2039), also stayed behind to support Central Command's retrograde. After the breakout of the 11th MEU (SOC), the remaining ships of PhibGru 3, led by the amphibious assault ship *Tarawa* (LHA 1), conducted routine maintenance in various Arabian Gulf ports and prepared for their redeployment. On 7 May, U.S. Naval Forces, Central Command, released PhibGru 3 and ordered it to return to the United States by way of the Indian Ocean and the Philippine Islands. PhibGru 3 was scheduled to come under the operational control of the Seventh Fleet on 10 May and could, if so ordered, be off the coast of Bangladesh seven days later.[31]

With the release of PhibGru 3 and the 5th MEB, the Pacific Command, which concurrently was considering and planning for a number of relief options, became convinced that using the task group's assets was the "best way to go" should the Department of Defense be directed to assist. Because of its inherent flexibility and capacity to react quickly, an amphibious task force was well-suited for relief operations in Bangladesh. The areas most in need of help were the offshore islands and the coastal lowlands, both of which were well within the reach of a landing force. It could easily provide needed transportation using landing craft, small boats, helicopters, and amphibious vehicles. Operations could be sea-based, hence, would require only minimal American forces on the shore, reducing the logistic demands on the fragile Bangladesh infrastructure.

As a result of the defense attache's query on the 6th, and subsequent discussions held between representatives of the command and Pacific Fleet, the Commander, Seventh Fleet requested the amphibious task group forward a "plan to provide immediate assistance including units to be diverted, proposed command structure, logistics support required, and ETA [estimated time of arrival] Chittagong area." Since the task group would be needed, according to embassy estimates, for two to three weeks, Seventh Fleet notified commanders of Naval Task Forces 76 and 73 that the potential existed that elements of Amphibious Ready Group Bravo, the amphibious cargo ship *St. Louis* (LKA 116), tank landing ship *San Bernardino* (LST 1189), or the Maritime Prepositioning Ship *First Lieutenant Jack Lummus* (TAK 3011), would be directed to relieve the amphibious task group on station. The task force commanders, like PhibGru 3, were to provide a coordinated plan of action, the

---

* The 2,000-man 11th MEU (SOC), composed of Battalion Landing Team 3/1, Marine Medium Helicopter Squadron 268, and Marine Service Support Group 11, had been embedded into the 5th MEB for Operation Desert Storm and was embarked on the *New Orleans* (LPH 11), *Denver* (LPD 9), *Mobile* (LKA 115), *Germantown* (LSD 42), and *Peoria* (LST 1183). Another PhibGru 3 ship, the *Tripoli* (LPH 10), struck a mine and was seriously damaged in January 1991.

earliest possible departure date for each ship, and estimated time of arrival off Chittagong.[32]

Responding to Seventh Fleet's request, PhibGru 3 reported that it could arrive the morning of 16 May, assuming a speed of 16 knots. Its planned concept of operations encompassed four main phases: a liaison visit between PhibGru 3 and 5th MEB personnel and relief officials at Chittagong; the airlift and surface movement of relief supplies and water-making facilities to pre-designated landing zones; the turnover of the relief mission to international agencies or follow-on relief organizations; and, finally, the return of personnel and equipment to their respective amphibious ships. Should the group be tasked with the relief mission, it requested appropriate radio frequencies, landing zone and distribution site locations, aeronautical and topographical charts, additional medical supplies and vaccines, especially against rabies, and the designation of specific liaison personnel from the Bangladesh navy and government or from a non-government relief organization.[33]

Task Force 76 reported that while a number of options were considered, it would recommend that the *St. Louis* proceed from Subic Bay in the Philippines to Okinawa where it would load a number of Marine Corps items best suited for relief operations such as reverse osmosis water purification units (ROWPUs), generators, and bulldozers.* From Okinawa, the *St. Louis* would steam to Chittagong, arriving about 23 May. The *San Bernardino* and *Lummus* would continue with their scheduled operations and not be deployed. This option, it noted, precluded any reliance on Military Airlift Command support and allowed adequate time to prestage the best humanitarian relief package from equipment available on Okinawa.[34] Seventh Fleet passed both the proposed recommendations of Task Force 76 and the concept of operations submitted by PhibGru 3 to CinCPac for consideration.

On the morning of 9 May, CinCPac informed Lieutenant Colonel Dunn that the command was closely monitoring the situation in Bangladesh and was taking a number of specific actions on his requests for assistance. The quantity and cost of chlorine-based water purification tablets and water cans were being identified. Thirteen pallets of relief and medical supplies, singled out by the Pacific Command's Humanitarian Assistance Office, were readied for shipment on Okinawa and would be airlifted by an Air Force Lockheed C-141 Starlifter to

---

* The Reverse Osmosis Water Purification Unit is a frame-mounted, portable water purification system capable of purifying water from almost any deep or shallow well or surface water source. The ROWPU is able to remove nuclear, biological, and chemical contaminants as well as minerals and biological impurities. The single greatest benefit of the reverse osmosis process is the ability to desalinate salt water. Powered by a 30-kilowatt generator, the ROWPU is capable of producing potable water at a rate of 600 gallons per hour.

The ROWPU's end product, drinkable water, posed a problem for many Bangladeshi. They could not comprehend how a machine, or a water purification tablet, could produce safe drinking water from water taken from poluted tube wells, and ponds or irrigation canals that had once contained the corpses of their livestock and countrymen.

Photograph courtesy of Shahidul Alam

A section of the damaged port of Chittagong illustrates the numerous wrecks which clogged the port, preventing ocean-going relief ships from delivering needed supplies.

Bangladesh on 10 May. Although the command informed Dunn that the closest helicopter assets were on board ships of the amphibious group and their use was "operationally preferred and logistically much more supportable" than drawing on air assets on Okinawa or in the Philippines, CinCPac noted that it could do nothing unless the group's diversion was requested and authorized. The same was true for Pacific Ocean Division Corps of Engineer personnel to be used in a damage assessment of Chittagong harbor and the use of communication personnel and equipment. Any CinCPac assistance was dependent upon the receipt of a specific American Embassy request and subsequent approval by the Chairman of the Joint Chiefs of Staff.[35]

In Bangladesh, the Office of Foreign Disaster Assistance notified the embassy that the Department of State had approved the requested allotment of an additional $4.25 million for disaster relief. USAID quickly obligated grants totalling more than $3.6 million with CARE, Save the Children Fund (USA), The Asia Foundation, World Vision, and a number of other non-government relief organizations. After receiving approval from the Bangladesh army, the embassy deployed the 15 soldiers from the U.S. Army's 84th Engineer Battalion to Chittagong to assist with the repair of the city's airport terminal and tower.[36]* Following the receipt of a request from the Bangladesh air force for additional parachutes to facilitate aerial delivery of relief supplies which

---

* The Army engineers did little in the terms of major reconstruction because construction materials were in very short supply and the availability of heavy engineer equipment was limited.

Lieutenant Colonel Dunn promptly forwarded to the Pacific Command for action, the defense attache, accompanied by several USAID officials, flew to Chittagong to continue damage reconnaissance.[37]

Upon their return to Dhaka and after subsequent discussions at the embassy, the mission's country team agreed that helicopters would be needed to perform relief operations. Accordingly, Ambassador Milam informed the Department of State of the recommendation on the 9th. Of the more than 5 million people severely affected by the cyclone, he reported, approximately half lived on islands or in coastal areas not served by main roads. The few feeder roads that existed were impassable and the island population was hard to reach due to rough seas and the shortage of large boats. The Bangladesh military, he noted, "has been able to reach these areas with relief goods intermittently by helicopter and occasional air drops . . . . You know better than I what an inexact science disaster assessment and assistance are." The ambassador concluded by noting that: "Our best judgement at this time, given humanitarian need, logistical difficulties of reaching island and remote mainland coastal areas, loss of BDG [Bangladesh government] helicopters and overuse of remaining ones, and need for newly elected government to perform well quickly is that U.S. supply of a few helicopters would be money well spent."[38]

At Ambassador Milam's request, Lieutenant Colonel Dunn advised CinCPac of the mission's "high interest in possible diversion" of the amphibious task group and asked "if earlier arrival was possible."[39] In response, CinCPac noted

The cyclone's fierce winds brought down several of the port's cranes, which hindered the relief efforts and placed a greater emphasis on the need for helicopter support.

Lieutenant Colonel Dunn concluded his appeal on behalf of the ambassador by requesting that "all attempts be made to make the *Tarawa* available for this noble mission."[44]

The Bangladesh government and American Embassy appeals were echoed by the United Nations. After meeting with private aid agencies in Dhaka, representatives of the world body declared "that foreign nations had failed to mount an effort sufficient to help the survivors of the cyclone." They concluded that "Bangladesh urgently needed helicopters, water purification tablets, tents, medical kits, plastic sheets, powdered milk and drugs, particularly anti-diarrhea medicine." The United Nations representatives considered the means of transporting these and other supplies to the cyclone victims essential.[45]

The repeated entreaties by Ambassador Milam and his staff for helicopter support had not gone unnoticed in Washington and Hawaii. On the 9th, following discussions between Deputy Secretary of State Lawrence S. Eagleburger, and Deputy and Acting Secretary of Defense Donald J. Atwood, the Department of State formally requested that the Department of Defense provide relief assistance in the form of heavy-lift helicopters, specifically those attached to the 5th Marine Expeditionary Brigade. The helicopters were to be used "to deliver relief supplies to low-lying coastal areas, flooded areas and areas not accessible by roads" for a period of approximately 14 days.[46] Shortly after 1700 on the 10th, Secretary Atwood forwarded a memorandum to the Chairman of the Joint Chiefs of Staff, General Colin L. Powell, directing "the commander in chief of the appropriate unified command or specified command to order appropriate elements of the Fifth Marine Expeditionary Brigade to make best speed to international waters adjacent to Bangladesh." The brigade's mission was to provide "transportation support to humanitarian relief efforts in Bangladesh." In a note appended to the memorandum, Secretary Atwood directed Major General Stackpole to Bangladesh to "assess and set up" communications and authorized a "speed up" of Amphibious Group 3.[47]

Late that evening, a warning order, prepared by the Joint Staff and approved by the Chairman, was sent to CinCPac requesting that Admiral Larson provide a "commander's estimate with alternative courses of action" for the President's consideration by noon on the 11th. The command was to be prepared, when directed by the President, to "provide support for relief operations to assist the Government of Bangladesh in recovering from tropical cyclone damage for a period of approximately 2 weeks." Authorized courses of action included--but were not limited to--providing helicopter lift of relief supplies, relief of Bangladesh government and U.S. Embassy personnel, search and rescue assistance, and communications help until the Bangladesh government could reestablish communications in the disaster area. Other commands, such as the Strategic Air and Special Operations Commands, were to provide appropriate support as required.[48]

Upon receipt of the warning order, CinCPac activated a crisis action team to address immediate and long-term assistance concerns. Working throughout the night, the team communicated its assessment and proposed concept of operations to the American Embassy in Dhaka and the Joint Staff in Washington early on the 11th. The established overriding priority was to assist in minimizing the death of additional Bangladeshi citizens in the postdisaster period. To that end, CinCPac proposed, when directed by the President, to execute a three-phase operation designed to provide command, control, and communications capability, "immediate short term disaster relief, and longer term sustainable humanitarian assistance to designated areas in Bangladesh."[49]

During phase one, a joint task force, codenamed Productive Effort, would be formed and the designated commander, Major General Stackpole, would deploy to Dhaka. He and his staff would establish liaison with the embassy's country team, officials of the Bangladesh government, private volunteer and international relief organizations, and would furnish CinCPac with an on-site mission assessment. To provide a means of assessment during phase two, CinCPac would deploy the first American rotary wing assets, consisting of five U.S. Army UH-60 Blackhawks, an environmental preventive medicine assessment capability, and a command, control, and communications augmentation cell. Following the assessment phases, the final phase would encompass an "organized, sustained effort to provide protracted humanitarian assistance." The Joint Task Force (JTF) commander would "direct and coordinate the relief efforts provided by light-, medium-, and heavy-lift

Department of Defense Photo (USAF) DF-ST-92-06107

MajGen Henry C. Stackpole III, commanding the III Marine Expeditionary Force headquartered on Okinawa, was given command of the joint American effort to provide disaster relief to the victims of the Bangladesh cyclone.

helicopters, surface and shallow draft craft and personnel" from Amphibious Group 3 and embarked 5th Marine Expeditionary Brigade. All activities would be limited to those permitted by the Department of State through the American ambassador to Bangladesh. In addition, CinCPac set a spending ceiling of $500,000, noting that service-incurred costs would be born by each obligating service.[50] "Rest assured," the Pacific Command informed the American Embassy, "USCinCPac is capable and prepared to respond with significant assets and speed to render appropriate assistance to our regional neighbors in Bangladesh."[51]

Moving rapidly, CinCPac activated Joint Task Force Productive Effort and formally designated Major General Henry C. Stackpole III, its commander. A Connecticut native, General Stackpole was commissioned a Marine second lieutenant in 1958 after his graduation from Princeton University. He served two tours in Vietnam and held command, staff, and school assignments before being appointed commanding general of the III Marine Expeditionary Force, 3d Marine Division, and Marine Corps Bases, Japan. He concurrently held the posts of Okinawa Area Coordinator under U.S. Forces, Japan, and Commander, Landing Force, Seventh Fleet. General Stackpole, as the Joint Task Force commander, was given operational control of all U.S. Air Force, Army, Navy, and Marine forces ashore or entering Bangladesh "to assist the Government of Bangladesh in recovering from tropical storm damage."[52] Deployment of the task force, however, would have to await an order from the President.

The Presidential order came early on 11 May. Based on the assessments and recommendations of the Departments of State and Defense and discussions between Deputy Secretary Eagleburger and National Security Advisor Brent Scowcroft, President Bush formally issued the order to dispatch the proposed joint task force to Bangladesh. In making the announcement, a White House spokesman noted that while the humanitarian effort would be "a significant contribution--in people and cost involved, . . . it is not unprecedented." Several recent examples were cited to support the use of American military personnel in humanitarian relief projects, such as aiding Kurdish refugees, and providing relief to victims of the San Francisco-area, Armenian, and Mexican earthquakes. "We have a long history of coming to the aid of people who need it," the spokesman said.[53]

Once the President approved the proposed disaster relief effort, the Secretary of Defense instructed CinCPac through the JCS to initiate Operation Productive Effort.[54] In the Philippines, General Stackpole received a call from the CinCPac J-3 (Operations) informing him that the President had decided to assist Bangladesh and inquired how soon he could be in Dhaka. Twenty-four hours, responded Stackpole.[55] General Stackpole and Colonel Lindblom immediately left Subic Bay and flew to Okinawa where he met with his staff, which had formed a crisis action team, at Camp Courtney. Already in contact with their counterparts at CinCPac and airlift traffic managers at Kadena Air Base on the island, the staff reported one C-141 Starlifter would be ready at 1800 that same evening, and that there would be limited ground and helicopter transport available for the survey and reconnaissance party upon its arrival in Dhaka. In addition, the staff had contacted the American defense attache about the current situation in Dhaka regarding water, food, transportation, shelter, electrical power, and security.[56] Lieutenant Colonel Dunn informed them that the situation in the capital was "normal," that a variety of accommodations were available, and that preliminary briefings by appropriate embassy staff and Bangladesh officials had been scheduled.[57] Given this information, Stackpole decided to go with a very small advance party, limited to no more than 30 Marine and Navy personnel, until the actual situation in Bangladesh could be ascertained. The remaining III MEF staff members would follow within 24 hours. Due to the absence of a military threat, few intelligence personnel would accompany the advance party or follow-on staff to Bangladesh. As CinCPac had directed the deployment of additional forces to augment the initial party and ordered PhibGru 3 to increase speed to 16 knots and proceed to a location in international waters off Chittagong, General Stackpole decided to wait and create a staff in Bangladesh that had a true joint character.[58]

Prior to their departure from Kadena, the 28-man advance party checked and adjusted mount-out boxes and field chests which held critical supplies and office equipment for operating in an expeditionary environment, updated their vaccinations, and made numerous other preparations necessitated by the short notice deployment. In addition, they "quickly ascertained that very little in the way of joint doctrine existed concerning humanitarian relief operations," noted Lieutenant Colonel Gary W. Anderson, so they "took an extensive file on OPERATION PROVIDE COMFORT."[59] The team carried enough food, water, and shelter to be self-supporting for the first 72 hours in-country, and included satellite communications equipment.[60] By 1800 on the 11th, the advance survey and reconnaissance party staged at Kadena Air Base.

At 2100, General Stackpole and the advance party left Kadena enroute to Dhaka with a scheduled stop at Utapao, Thailand. While refueling at Utapao, a problem of overflight rights for Burma and India arose. Due to the short notice, emergency nature of the mission and the fact that the flight was taking place on a weekend, both countries refused to grant permission for the aircraft to proceed. "I had to make a hard decision leaving Utapao, Thailand as to whether we were going to have fighters scrambled to come after us from India or not," Stackpole later recounted. Despite the lack of clearance, Stackpole decided to press on, informing both countries that the mission was "for humanitarian purposes." Skirting their air defense network "to the extent we could," the flight proceeded on to Dhaka without incident.[61*]

---

* Burma required diplomatic clearance for Stackpole's aircraft and all follow-on Military Airlift Command (MAC) aircraft prior to granting flight clearance through the Yangon flight information region. Since the proposed route did not come within 12 nautical miles of Burmese territory, no diplomatic clearances were requested by the U.S. Because of the lack of clearances, MAC aircraft experienced numerous delays. To avoid the delays, aircrews filed flight plans that skirted the Yangon flight information region.

Marshalling the Forces

Early on the morning of 12 May, the Air Force C-141 Starlifter carrying Major General Stackpole and the advance party broke through a heavy layer of clouds and began its final approach into Zia International Airport outside Dhaka. The aircraft touched down shortly before 0700 and taxied to the airport's main terminal. General Stackpole was greeted by Ambassador Milam, Lieutenant Colonel Dunn, and members of the country team, as well as a delegation of Bangladesh officials that included State Minister of Relief and Rehabilitation, Luftur Rahman Khan; Chief of the General Staff, Major General Abdus Salam; and other general officers from the government's Supreme Command Headquarters. Following their arrival, General Stackpole and the primary members of his staff drove into Dhaka, dropped off their gear at the government's guest house in the Dhaka Cantonment, adjacent to Army Headquarters, and then moved on to a breakfast meeting with the ambassador, the defense attache, and senior embassy and USAID officials. The remainder of the advance party was billeted temporarily in an embassy-leased house on the outskirts of the capital not far from the American Club.[62]

Stackpole and the senior members of his team spent the morning being briefed by the ambassador and embassy personnel and the afternoon receiving an update of the situation and ongoing relief efforts from Bangladesh military and civilian officials and representatives of several non-government relief organizations. Despite the gallant efforts of the Bangladesh government and military, all reported that the situation was bleak and required immediate action. "My initial impression," General Stackpole told Admiral Larson that evening, "is that although the situation is grave, the immediate threat posed by the situation, such as dehydration, starvation, and injury, can be dealt with in the stipulated 14-day time frame. However, estimate considerable assistance needed to stabilize health crisis will be required for an additional 14 days. The Bangladesh military is providing heroic support within capabilities, but desperately needs help to do so successfully." The "Ambassador and staff," he concluded, "have rendered superb support and briefings in helping us get our feet on the ground."[63]

Stackpole and his staff met to review a number of common observations and to work on a preliminary assessment of the situation which would be relayed to CinCPac. By the time of the meeting, Stackpole had assumed operational control of the U.S. Army's 84th Engineer Battalion detachment, and combat camera, public affairs, and maintenance personnel from the on-going Cobra Gold exercise in Thailand who were also assigned to augment the Joint Task Force. A Disaster Assessment and Relief Team (DART) from the 1st Battalion, 1st Special Forces Group A (Airborne), which was flown from Okinawa via the Philippines on board two Air Force Lockheed HC-130 Hercules aircraft belonging to the 17th

Photograph courtesy of American Embassy, Bangladesh

American Ambassador William B. Milan, left, MajGen Henry C. Stackpole III, and LtGen Muhammad Noor Uddin Khan, chief of staff of the Bangladeshi army, were briefed during the preparatory stage of the relief operation.

Special Operations Squadron, 353d Special Operations Wing, was also chopped to the Joint Task Force.* The Special Operations Force commander, Lieutenant Colonel George W. Norwood, USAF, was designated the Special Operations component commander and attended the late evening meeting.[64]

Briefings by Bangladesh, embassy, and non-government relief agency representatives provided Stackpole and the Joint Task Force staff with an accurate picture of the situation. The most pressing relief effort problem was the prioritization of existing aid supplies and their distribution. The task force staff agreed that neither the massive use of ground forces, nor a large influx of relief supplies would be needed. The quantity of food, especially grain, stored in government and non-government relief organizations' warehouses was considered adequate to meet the emergency. With the road network virtually destroyed and the affected area covered by shallow water, only helicopters, air-cushion landing

---

* The DART was task organized from 1st Battalion, 1st Special Forces Group with the command and control element and an advanced operational base composed of a Special Forces Operational Detachment Bravo and two Special Forces Operational Detachment Alphas. The team was composed of 36 Special Operations personnel, including command and control, operations, intelligence, logistics, communications, medical, and weather personnel.

A third aircraft, a C-130 from the 1st Special Operations Squadron, carrying additional Joint Task Force command and special tactics team personnel was forced to remain in Thailand when the aircraft developed a main landing gear malfunction.

craft (LCAC), air drops, and the limited use of conventional landing craft could be used. As General Stackpole stated to CinCPac: "We will deliver food, water and supplies to GOB [Government of Bangladesh] Forces in place for immediate distribution to [the] population to preserve life."[65]

General Stackpole, in his preliminary assessment, reported two major concerns. The first, shared by Ambassador Milam, was "to avoid the appearance of stepping in to relieve the government." The newly elected democratic government, Stackpole noted, was trying hard to cope with the unprecedented disaster and its sovereign right to lead the relief effort had to be respected. America's operational control rather than command would be emphasized.[66] "Believe it important," he continued, "that we be visibly working hand in hand with the GOB [Government of Bangladesh] and Bangladesh military as a team." Stackpole's philosophy from the outset "was to 'backbone' the gallant Bangladesh efforts rather than be intrusive or overwhelming in demands on the fragile infrastructure of this third world nation."[67] He considered it vital that the government be in charge of the relief effort and that a coordinating mechanism be created which would bring all agencies involved together and to work toward a common end. The arrival of the amphibious task group, he noted, would be "invaluable due to their ability to operate in a sea-based mode. This sea-based presence will also help us avoid further stressing an already strained national infra-structure."[68]

Stackpole's second concern was for needed medical support. Abysmal sanitary conditions and the resultant contamination of the affected area's water supply would produce, he surmised, more deaths from disease than from starvation or dehydration. Although follow-on medical teams would be needed, he stressed that the distribution of food and water was the primary focus of the effort. "Overall," he concluded, "[I] am confident that forces currently planned can alleviate immediate crisis as it exists in next 14 days." However, an "end state" eventually would need to be defined in coordination with the American ambassador, CinCPac, and the Joint Chiefs of Staff "to ensure that we do not appear to be an 'occupying force' in the long run. Currently envision providing immediate lifesaving response for 14 days and follow on support as required for a further 14 if NCA [National Command Authorities] requires. Currently do not envision presence beyond that."[69]

Stackpole's preliminary distribution plan involved transport of food and supplies by fixed-wing aircraft from Dhaka to Chittagong, about 190 kilometers south of the capital. Relief supplies would then be delivered from Chittagong to the outlying coastal areas and islands by helicopter and surface craft. Until regular Air Force C-130s capable of carrying larger payloads arrived, General Stackpole proposed using the two Special Operations HC-130 aircraft for the initial runs between Dhaka and Chittagong. The five UH-60 Blackhawk helicopters and crews from the 4th Battalion, 25th Aviation Regiment of the U.S. Army Pacific's 25th Infantry Division, accompanying the Joint Task Force augmentation cell from Hawaii, where to be designated the initial primary rotary wing delivery platforms. Upon the arrival of Amphibious Group 3 with Marine

Aircraft Group 50's 26 medium- and heavy-lift helicopters on 15 May, the 5th MEB would assume the main burden of distributing relief supplies to inaccessible areas within the disaster zone.

Before submitting a formal assessment and detailed campaign plan to CinCPac for approval, General Stackpole wanted to make a visual reconnaissance of the disaster area.* The visit was scheduled for early the following morning so as to be completed by midday, before the eruption of daily afternoon thunderstorms which could make flying difficult. Stackpole's initial survey would stress the requirements needed to reopen Chittagong airport for routine flight operations, in addition to looking for unflooded landing zones, landing craft ramp sites, and secure areas where reverse osmosis water purification units could be set up.[70]

At 0800 on 13 May, Stackpole and the senior members of his staff met with Lieutenant General Muhammad Noor Uddin Khan, Chief of Staff of the Bangladesh Army, Ambassador Milam, Director Kilgour, and key members of the Bangladesh Supreme Command staff. Following a short meeting they boarded two Bangladesh air force UH-1 Huey helicopters for an extensive tour of the disaster area. Stops included Chittagong city and airport, Sandwip, South Hatia, Kutubdia, and Maheshkali Islands. "The devastation was extremely sobering," noted the Joint Task Force commander.[71] "I have seen combat," but "I have never seen greater carnage." As he later recalled:

> It dwarfed anything that happened in Desert Storm. And because the total infrastructure was destroyed in these outlying islands and up to five kilometers inland along this 110 mile coastline, there was no way to bury [the dead] in mass graves or even be able to get out into the area and get control of the situation. All communications were knocked out. Water supplies . . . were completely polluted by this point in time. The toxicity of the bodies, now bloated, was a serious problem for us. People were dying of cholera. They were dying of a variety of other diseases. Simple scratches had become infected; amputations were legion. We had many, many problems which to solve.[72]

The devastation, Stackpole reported, "imbued all concerned with [a] renewed sense of purpose concerning the absolutely vital need for relief operations." The tour also confirmed his belief that the distribution of water, food, and supplies would be the main focus of the Joint Task Force's relief effort. With adequate

---

* On 12 May, the embassy sent a liaison team to Chittagong in order to coordinate the effort and to prepare for Stackpole's visit. The presence of embassy personnel in Chittagong proved to be "extraordinarily useful and essential" as the operation progressed. (Jon F. Danilowicz, Comments on draft ms, 18Feb95)

Photograph courtesy of USCinCPac

One of five U.S. Army Blackhawk helicopters from the 4th Battalion, 25th Aviation Regiment, based in Hawaii, is unloaded at Zia International Airport. The helicopters were part of the Joint Task Force augmentation cell.

food supplies available, the problem would be getting it to the areas where it was needed due to the destroyed infrastructure.[73]

Shortly after General Stackpole's return to Dhaka, the Air Force C-5A Galaxy transport carrying five U.S. Army Blackhawk helicopters, support equipment, and the 56-man augmentation cell arrived from Hawaii.[74] The cell was composed of helicopter support, communications, and public affairs personnel, and the initial elements of the Navy's Environmental and Preventive Medicine Unit 6 (NEPMU 6). In addition, it included the Joint Task Force's deputy commander, Colonel Edward G. Hoffman, USAF. He also was designated the JTF Air Force component commander. Lieutenant Colonel Thomas F. Elzey, USA, in command of the Blackhawk detachment, was named the JTF Army component commander. While welcome, the cell lacked standing operating procedures and competent personnel to deal with administrative, automated data processing, contracting, purchasing, and comptroller matters.* While separate elements of the cell had trained for such deployments, the cell as a whole was not prepared.

---

* The Pacific Command eventually deployed professional personnel from Hawaii and Okinawa, but in the interim the embassy lent a number of staff members to assist the JTF in the areas of public affairs, legal, public health, and contracting.

As the staff continued to grow, a tentative headquarters site was identified at Tezgaon, the old international airport midway between Dhaka and Zia International. The unused Bangladesh air force barracks at Tezgaon was selected, as it was not far from the Presidential Secretariat building which housed the civil-military team formed by the Bangladesh government to manage the relief effort. The barracks soon proved unsuitable as a JTF Operations Center due to its small, compartmented rooms which separated principal staff sections, hindering the flow of information within the staff and to higher headquarters and component commanders.

The embassy and the American International School provided accommodations at no cost for the staff. "Our living situation is much better that we had anticipated," wrote Lieutenant Colonel James L. White, USAF, commander of a contingent of the 374th Tactical Airlift Wing from Yokota Air Base, Japan. "We live on the second floor of the embassy Storage and Furniture Warehouse. It is air conditioned and we have used our [own] cots and their mattresses. We have outdoor showers and a small embassy commissary, which

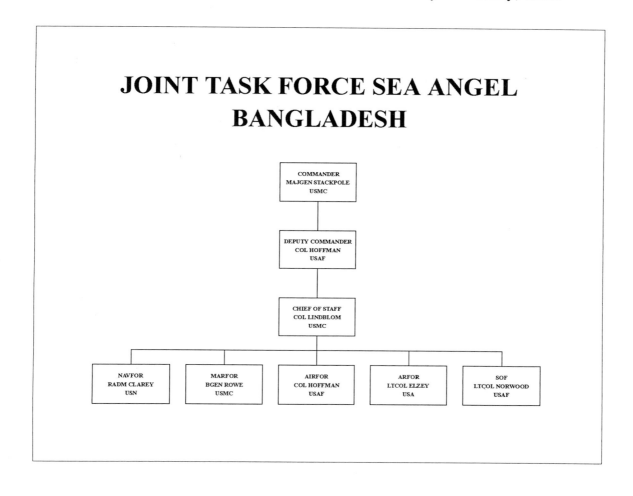

JOINT TASK FORCE SEA ANGEL BANGLADESH

COMMANDER
MAJGEN STACKPOLE
USMC

DEPUTY COMMANDER
COL HOFFMAN
USAF

CHIEF OF STAFF
COL LINDBLOM
USMC

| NAVFOR RADM CLAREY USN | MARFOR BGEN ROWE USMC | AIRFOR COL HOFFMAN USAF | ARFOR LTCOL ELZEY USA | SOF LTCOL NORWOOD USAF |

helps a lot. We eat MREs [Meals Ready to Eat] except for dinner, which is a hot meal provided by the American Club."[75] In addition, the embassy loaned support equipment such as copying machines and air conditioners, allowed the JTF to requisition office supplies and other items from the General Service Office store, and provided local transportation and laundry service on a reimbursable basis.[76]

Late in the day, General Stackpole again met with Ambassador Milam and senior Ministry of Relief officials and military officers in charge of relief operations. A number of Bangladeshis present expressed concern as to the JTF's resources and how they would be used. Following an explanation by General Stackpole of the task force's mission, resources, and proposed role in the relief effort, and Ambassador Milam's reassurances, apprehension slowly gave way to guarded support.[77]

Based on his personal observations, discussions with Bangladesh officials and members of the embassy's country team, and political and geographical realities, Stackpole decided to split the JTF staff between Chittagong and Dhaka. Colonel Stephen Lindblom, III MEF operations officer, would remain in Dhaka as the Joint Task Force's Chief of Staff with Marine Lieutenant Colonel Gary W. Anderson as his operations officer. Located in the capital near government ministries and the country's only major airport, the Dhaka center would function primarily as a planning and liaison headquarters. In addition it would co-ordinate--in consultation with representatives of the Bangladesh government, American embassy, other foreign military contingents and embassies, and non-government relief agencies--incoming aid, the staging of relief materials, and the setting of priorities for flights to forward areas. With few exceptions, all air and sea assets contributed to the relief effort by other foreign governments were placed under the JTF's operational control. The Chittagong center, situated at the city's Patenga Airport, would schedule helicopter flights and landing craft operations to move the relief supplies to outlying islands and coastal areas within the disaster zone. The center would not only act as a transshipment point, but also as the local coordination center for civilian, Bangladeshi, and foreign military forces engaged in the relief effort. Air Force Colonel Mike Ferguson was designated the chief of staff for Joint Task Force (Forward) (JTF Forward) headquarters at Chittagong. Navy Captain Edward P. Anglim from Amphibious Group 1 became his operations officer. General Stackpole and Colonel Hoffman planned to rotate between the two centers, providing constant command presence.[78]

After his inspection tour, General Stackpole forwarded an update of the situation to CinCPac and requested additional communications and airlift support. At that time, the only voice communications among Dhaka, Okinawa, and Hawaii was the portable, single-channel, ultra-high-frequency PSC-3 satellite communications terminal carried by the advance party. The lack of a high-gain tactical satellite antenna, unstable local power, and harsh environmental conditions initially limited the system's effectiveness. Although Army Special Forces brought long-range communications equipment and quickly established a

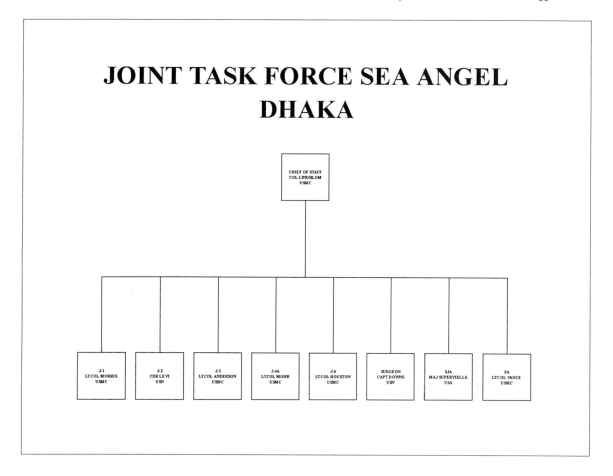

JOINT TASK FORCE SEA ANGEL
DHAKA

CHIEF OF STAFF
COL LINDBLOM
USMC

| J-1 LTCOL MORRIS USMC | J-2 CDR LE VI USN | J-3 LTCOL ANDERSON USMC | J-4A LTCOL MOHR USMC | J-6 LTCOL HOUSTON USMC | SURGEON CAPT DOWNS USN | SJA MAJ SUPERVIELLE USA | PA LTCOL VANCE USMC |

functioning net, it rapidly was overburdened. Hard-copy (non-voice) message traffic had to be relayed through the embassy's message center. Although the JTF had access to the host country's limited civilian and military telephone service between Dhaka and Chittagong, the establishment of reliable command, disaster relief, and air traffic control nets, in addition to "Autodin" and "Autovon" support for the disaster control centers, was "critical to operations," Stackpole reported.[*] He also requested four more Air Force C-130 transports and the necessary command and support packages to provide adequate intra-theater lift. His immediate priorities were: to establish the forward headquarters at Chittagong; place Special Operations assessment teams at six Bangladesh military relief sites; position water purification units at about a dozen secure locations; and begin relief and reconnaissance flights as soon as possible. "Every

---

[*] The Automatic Voice Network (Autovon) and Automatic Digital Network (Autodin) are the principal long-haul voice and digital communications networks within the Defense Communications System.

effort," he emphasized, "is being made to conduct assessment and follow-on op[eration]s in conjunction with Bangladesh civil and military authorities. . . . Believe JTF can make real and immediate impact on efforts to reduce mortality and stabilize the situation almost immediately."[79]

General Stackpole followed up his assessment with a more detailed concept of operations for Phase I of the campaign plan developed by the CinCPac crisis action team. The goal of the on-going first phase was to take immediate action to minimize mortality and stabilize the situation by overcoming the recurring problem of distribution. "In doing so," Stackpole said, "we must maximize cross support until we reach a point where the whole effort is greater than the sum of [its parts]." Beginning on 15 May, the forward operations center would be activated at Chittagong airport and begin relief operations in the hardest-hit areas. In addition, communications teams and water purification units would be located at key Bangladesh army relief centers. To facilitate the aid effort, each service component of the joint command would be assigned an individual sector based on its available assets, for the distribution of food and relief supplies. The northern sector, encompassing the coastal region north of the Karnaphuli River, was assigned to the Army component; the Marine component was given the southern sector, the coastal area south of the Karnaphuli River, centered on Cox's Bazar and Kutubdia Island; and the island sector, which incorporated Sandwip, North and South Hatia, and Manpura Islands, as well as the smaller surrounding mud flats, was allotted to the Navy component. The Special Operations and Air Force components were to provide assessment and airlift support as required.[80]

Taking Stackpole's assessment, the operational concept, Task Force 76's recommendation, and the amphibious task group's projected 14-day commitment into consideration, CinCPac suggested that the St. Louis, instead of the Maritime Prepositioning Ship Lummus, relieve the Navy task group and embarked Marine brigade. Pacific Command's recommendation was based upon the size and nature of the cargo and the existing harbor conditions at Chittagong. On the 13th, Seventh Fleet ordered the St. Louis, under the command of Captain John W. Peterson, to proceed from Subic Bay in the Philippines to Naha, Okinawa. At Naha, the St. Louis would load 28 reverse osmosis water purification units (ROWPUs), each weighing more than five tons, for use in the relief effort. Another eight units would be airlifted to Bangladesh. The amphibious cargo ship was scheduled to depart Okinawa on the 19th and arrive off Chittagong 10 days later. There she would replace the amphibious task group, which then would resume its return voyage to the West Coast. The Lummus was placed on alert status should the ship be needed.[81]

To support the deployment and use of the water purification units and assist with the humanitarian effort, III MEF activated Contingency Marine Air-Ground Task Force 2-91 (CMAGTF 2-91).[82] Drawn from 26 different MEF units, the contingency air-ground task force was composed of a command element from the 9th Marine Expeditionary Brigade, a ground element drawn from Company F, 2d Battalion, 23d Marines, and a combat service support element consisting of

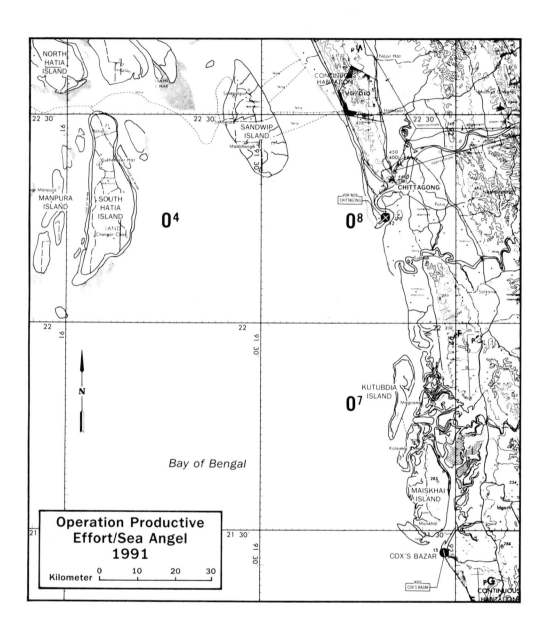

Operation Productive
Effort/Sea Angel
1991

Kilometer 0   10   20   30

Department of Defense Photo (USAF) DF-ST-92-06142

U.S. Air Force TSgt K. L. Jones, a member of a Mobile Area Assessment Team, coordinates Joint Task Force relief efforts with CARE personnel on Kutubdia Island.

medical, engineer, motor transport, supply, and maintenance detachments from the 3d Force Service Support Group.* The Marine task force included no aviation combat element. Within 96 hours of activation, 44 Marines and Navy corpsmen, with the eight ROWPUs, generators, floodlights, and associated equipment, had been airlifted to Bangladesh, moved to their designated locations, and were producing potable water. On the 19th, the remaining 190 Marines, in addition to medical and repair parts packages worth more than $1 million, embarked on board the *St. Louis* and departed Okinawa for Bangladesh.[83]

On 14 May, as Major General Stackpole, Ambassador Milam, Lieutenant General Noor Uddin Khan, and others continued their reconnaissance of the affected area, the vanguard of JTF Forward headquarters deployed to Chittagong. Units included Special Operations Force personnel organized as Mobile Area Assessment Teams. These teams were positioned at key Bangladesh relief sites throughout the mainland and offshore islands. The small, three- to four-man teams were composed of a communications specialist, medical technician, engineer, and at times a team leader, and were accompanied by two Bangladesh soldiers. The teams: conducted an area assessment; selected and, to a limited degree, secured helicopter landing zones; established long-range communications;

---

* 2d Battalion, 23d Marines, was a Selected Marine Reserve unit headquartered at Encino, California. The battalion was mobilized in December 1990 and deployed to Okinawa to fill the depleted ranks of the 9th Marines.

ANGELS FROM THE SEA: RELIEF OPERATIONS IN BANGLADESH, 1991

administered limited medical and disaster assistance; and coordinated follow-on or supporting relief efforts, noting any specific medical, food, water, or equipment needs. It was only after the deployment and subsequent debriefing of these teams, as General Stackpole later noted, "that the Bangladeshi had the full impact and magnitude of what had occurred."[84] In addition to the Special Forces teams, Air Force specialists from the 1723d Special Tactics Squadron were tasked to do assessments of the airfields at Chittagong, Cox's Bazar, and Dhaka to determine their load-bearing capabilities.

As the day wore on, the remaining elements of the CinCPac augmentation cell arrived in Dhaka and were quickly integrated into the JTF staff or supporting component units. The forces included additional Army Blackhawk aviators and support personnel, a six-man reserve civil affairs team from the 351st Civil Affairs Command, a Corps of Engineers harbor assessment team, and communications, public affairs, and medical staff.[*] Among the later group was Captain John R. Downs, MC, USNR, who was designated the JTF surgeon.

The following day, preparations for the expanded international relief effort moved into high gear. In Dhaka, as the Agency for International Development continued to expedite the relief effort by extending additional grants to several non-government agencies, the JTF staff continued to work on the campaign plan, which would be forwarded to CinCPac once it received planning input from the amphibious task force. In addition, the staff collaborated with members of the Bangladesh government's civil and military relief team and representatives of major non-government organizations to build a national-level coordinating committee to establish priorities. The first meeting of the national committee took place on the 15th to set the priorities for the following day as to the type and quantity of relief supplies airlifted to Chittagong. Chaired by Bangladesh army Brigadier Shafaat Ahmed, charged by Prime Minister Zia with responsibility for the relief effort, the committee included representatives from the JTF, U.S. Agency for International Development, Bangladesh military, government civil agencies, and several non-government relief organizations such as the Red Crescent Society and CARE. The national coordinating committee met daily until 28 May when it was determined that an adequate amount of relief supplies had been delivered to Chittagong. Future meetings would only be called when needed.

Also on the 15th, JTF Forward headquarters was formally established at Chittagong with the arrival of additional American military and embassy

----

[*] The civil affairs team was to assist in coordination efforts among the Government of Bangladesh, non-government relief organizations, American Embassy, and U.S. military forces. As a member of the team, native-born Sergeant First Class Faruque U. Ahmed returned to Bangladesh a hero. However, he did not view himself as such. "I'm just a soldier doing my job," he said. "I'm just happy to get an opportunity to do something good for my homeland." (Maj John R. Spotts, USAR, "Operation Sea Angel: USCINCPAC Responds," *Asia-Pacific Defense Forum*, Fall 1991, p. 44.)

personnel and the first relief supplies on board a Special Forces HC-130 from Dhaka. Organized on short notice and consisting primarily of senior officers, the forward headquarters had few clerks, little in the way of administrative supplies and equipment, and no cots, water cans, or other "camp" supplies. Although initially "small in number and shallow in density," as the 5th MEB's commanding officer later noted, the Chittagong forward headquarters would become the major player in the relief effort.[85]

With the establishment of the headquarters, the first meeting between government civilian, military, and non-government organization representatives and members of the JTF took place. As a result of the meeting, the Chittagong Coordination Cell was formed, co-chaired by government secretary and zonal relief coordinator M. Mokammel Haque and Marine Colonel Russell F. Bailes, Jr.[86]

Prior to the arrival of the JTF, distribution of relief supplies within Chittagong and Cox's Bazar districts had been coordinated separately by each of the agencies involved, without an agreed focus of effort. The joint coordination cell would provide the needed focus and ensure optimum use of the task force's transportation assets in the distribution of relief supplies. The cell was located at the Patenga Airport recruit training school facility and was composed of representatives of the JTF, Bangladesh government, 24th Bangladesh Army Division, and several non-government organizations. The cell established a prioritized list of relief supplies to be transported: (1) food, water, and medical supplies; (2) clothing; (3) shelter and building supplies; and (4) tube well supplies, power pumps, and piping. Based on this list of priorities, the cell planned and scheduled the movement of supplies by helicopter or surface craft. Requests for emergency supply or personnel lift had to involve a life-threatening situation, and if validated, would be scheduled for immediate movement. In addition, the cell established relief supply delivery sites within each of the districts included inside the Chittagong Disaster Zone. Initially, these sites would be under government control in order to provide crowd control and protection for the surface craft and helicopters.[87]

As the forward headquarters became operational, it assumed control of the two squads of Army engineers and the five Army Blackhawk helicopters, deployed to Chittagong to support the positioning of the first of several Special Forces Mobile Area Assessment Teams to the outlying islands. The forward headquarters tasked these assessment and communications teams with providing assistance to the Chittagong cell in determining relief effort requirements. The teams took with them the first relief supplies transported to a designated disaster site. In addition to distributing the first relief supplies, JTF Forward attempted to provide emergency medical care, but found that it was beyond the capabilities of its limited aid station.[88] A majority of the first day's activities, however, was directed toward preparing for the arrival and subsequent deployment of the amphibious task force composed of Amphibious Group 3 and the 5th Marine Expeditionary Brigade.

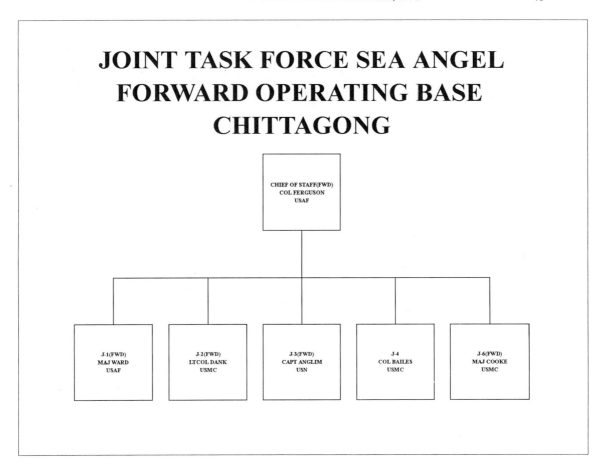

JOINT TASK FORCE SEA ANGEL FORWARD OPERATING BASE CHITTAGONG

CHIEF OF STAFF(FWD)
COL FERGUSON
USAF

| J-1(FWD) MAJ WARD USAF | J-2(FWD) LTCOL DANK USMC | J-3(FWD) CAPT ANGLIM USN | J-4 COL BAILES USMC | J-6(FWD) MAJ COOKE USMC |

PhibGru3 was composed of seven amphibious ships and one support ship: the general purpose amphibious assault ship *Tarawa* (LHA 1); the amphibious transport docks *Vancouver* (LPD 2) and *Juneau* (LPD 10); the dock landing ships *Anchorage* (LSD 36) and *Mount Vernon* (LSD 39); the tank landing ships *Frederick* (LST 1184) and *Barbour County* (LST 1195); and the fleet oiler *Passumpsic* (T-AO 107). The amphibious group's landing craft included four air cushioned landing craft, utility and mechanized landing craft, and both inflatable and rigid raiding craft.[89]

Rear Admiral Stephen S. Clarey commanded the eight-ship, 3,000-man amphibious group. A native of Hawaii, Admiral Clarey graduated from Williams College before attending Naval Officer Candidate School in 1962. Trained at various Navy schools and a veteran of Vietnam service, Clarey previously had commanded the tank landing ship *Suffolk County* (LST 1173), destroyer *Elliot* (DD 967), and Destroyer Squadron 21. In addition to his shipboard assignments, Clarey had held a number of service and joint staff positions before assuming command of PhibGru3 in March 1990. He also commanded the Maritime Prepositioning Force in Southwest Asia during Operation Desert Shield.

Department of Defense Photo (USAF) DO-307-SPT-91-7071

When the first U.S. Army Blackhawk helicopters arrive at landing zones on Sandwip Island they are rapidly unloaded and the relief supplies quickly distributed.

The 4,000-man 5th MEB, as all Marine air-ground task forces, had four elements: a command element, a ground combat element, an aviation combat element, and a combat service support element.* The brigade headquarters, reinforced with reconnaissance, intelligence, communications, and military police personnel, was the command element. The ground combat element was Regimental Landing Team 5 (RLT 5), commanded by Colonel Randolph A. Gangle. Marine Aircraft Group 50 (MAG-50), commanded by Colonel Randall L. West, was the aviation combat element. Brigade Service Support Group 5 (BSSG 5), commanded by Major Robert G. Johnson, provided logistic support.[90]

The 5th MEB's commanding general was Brigadier General Peter J. Rowe. Born in Connecticut, General Rowe graduated from Xavier University in Cincinnati, Ohio, and received a master's degree from San Diego State University. During 30 years' service, he had commanded almost every sized infantry unit, and had been assistant division commander of the 1st Marine Division prior to assuming command of the 5th MEB. In May 1990, he was

---

* Formed at Camp Pendleton in October 1990, the 5th MEB sailed for the Persian Gulf where it was assigned to the Marine Forces Afloat, later became I Marine Expeditionary Force reserve ashore, participated in combat actions at the Ice Cube and Ice Tray and the Al Wafrah Forest in Kuwait, and then backloaded to sail for home. The "embedded" 11th Marine Expeditionary Unit (SOC), which comprised about one-third of the brigade's strength, was detached on 16 March 1991 and remained in the Arabian Gulf until July 1991.

"dual-hatted" as the commanding general of both the Landing Force Training Command, Pacific, and the 5th MEB.

The 5th MEB could muster a solid nucleus for humanitarian operations. The brigade command element possessed a staff well-versed in rapid planning and had good communications assets. RLT 5 was ready to send headquarters staff, liaison officers, volunteer laborers, transportation assets, and supplies ashore. MAG-50's inventory included medium-lift transport helicopters, heavy-lift cargo helicopters, and light utility helicopters. BSSG 5, although stripped of a majority of its assets with the departure of the 11th Marine Expeditionary Unit (MEU), could provide water-production units, portable electric generators, trucks, forklifts, and other engineer resources.[91]

Brigade headquarters included 400 personnel and was composed of Headquarters and Service Company and the 5th Surveillance, Reconnaissance, and Intelligence Support Group (5th SRISG). The 5th SRISG was specifically organized to provide intelligence support for the 5th MEB and included detachments from 1st Radio Battalion, 4th Force Reconnaissance Company, 9th Communications Battalion, and a military police detachment.

RLT 5 was built around two battalions of the 5th Marines and an artillery battalion from Camp Pendleton, reinforced by combat support units composed of both active duty Marines and Reserve. The landing team included: Headquarters Company, 5th Marines; 2d Battalion, 5th Marines; 3d Battalion, 5th Marines; 2d Battalion, 11th Marines; Company B, 1st Reconnaissance

Department of Defense Photo (USN) DN-ST-90-05672

The Tarawa-*led seven-ship Amphibious Group 3, with the embarked 5th Marine Expeditionary Brigade, which deployed from the Persian Gulf to the Bay of Bengal to assist with the relief effort.*

Battalion; Company A, 4th Tank Battalion, a Reserve unit from Miramar, California; Company A, 4th Assault Amphibian Battalion, a Reserve unit from Norfolk, Virginia; Company A, 4th Combat Engineer Battalion, a Reserve unit from Charleston, West Virginia; and Company B, 1st Combat Engineer Battalion.

The aviation combat element was MAG-50, which was composed of Marine Medium Helicopter Squadron 265 (HMM-265) from Kaneohe, Hawaii; Marine Light Attack Helicopter Squadron 169 (HMLA-169) from Camp Pendleton; Detachment B, Marine Attack Squadron 513 (VMA-513) from Yuma, Arizona; Detachment A, Marine Heavy Helicopter Squadron 772 (HMH-772), a Reserve unit from Alameda Naval Air Station, California; 3d Low Altitude Air Defense Battalion (3d LAAD) from Camp Pendleton; a detachment from Marine Wing Support Squadron 372 (MWSS-372) from Camp Pendleton; and a detachment from Marine Air Support Squadron 6 (MASS-6), South Weymouth, Massachusetts.* The aircraft available included 12 Boeing CH-46E Sea Knights (HMM-265), 4 Sikorsky RH-53D Sea Stallions (HMH-772), 10 Bell UH-1Ns (HMLA-169), 7 Bell AH-1W Sea Cobras (HMLA-169), and 6 McDonnell Douglas AV-8B Harriers (VMA-513).** PhibGru3 carried two Sikorsky SH-3H Sea King night-capable, search and rescue (SAR) helicopters.***

According to Lieutenant Colonel Richard T. Kohl, who commanded Marine Service Support Group 24 during Operation Provide Comfort, the international humanitarian relief operation in northern Iraq, Marine combat service support elements were perfectly suited for humanitarian operations because of their special equipment and expeditionary nature. This was especially true for BSSG 5. BSSG 5 was formed at Camp Pendleton, California. Its nucleus was composed of stay-behind cadre when the 1st Force Service Support Group (1st FSSG) left for the Persian Gulf to support I Marine Expeditionary Force. These cadres merged with recently activated units of the Selected Marine Corps Reserve in late November. BSSG 5's muster rolls comprised engineers, mechanics,

---

* Four aircraft from HMH-772 joined MAG-50 on board the *Tarawa* from the Naval Air Facility, Jubayl, Saudi Arabia, in anticipation of being needed for the Ethiopian evacuation. Due to heavy ship loading conditions, the unit was authorized to bring only those personnel necessary for minimum flight operations. The shortage of maintenance personnel to service the four RH-53Ds subsequently strained the supply and maintenance support for these Sea Stallions during the relief effort in Bangladesh.

** The Sikorsky RH-53Ds were similar in appearance to CH-53Ds, but had twin T64-GE-415 engines and automatic flight controls for sustained low-level flight. Four of the UH-1Ns were grounded due to structural weaknesses that required depot repair work.

*** The SH-3H is an anti-submarine warfare (ASW) helicopter. The ASW systems had been removed from these aircraft and they were deployed specifically as night SAR helicopters, the first such deployment in the Navy, and a precursor to removing the ill-suited, organic Navy UN-1Ns and subsequent deployment of HH-46 SAR helicopter detachments on board amphibious assault ships. (RAdm Stephen S. Clarey, Comments on draft ms, 23Feb95)

drivers, forklift operators, communicators, medics, fuel handlers, and other specialists. Its equipment included 14 forklifts, 10 water purification units, 10 portable generators, 8 motorcycles, 7 bulldozers, and 16 five-ton trucks.

Major Robert G. Johnson commanded BSSG 5. Its elements included detachments from Headquarters and Service Battalions, 1st and 4th FSSGs; 1st Landing Support Battalion; 6th Motor Transport Battalion (Lubbock, Texas); 6th Engineer Support Battalion (Battle Creek, Michigan); 1st and 4th Supply Battalions; 1st and 4th Maintenance Battalions; 1st Medical Battalion; 1st Dental Battalion; and 6th and 7th Communications Battalions. The main drawback was that the brigade service support group was short of personnel. It originally sailed from San Diego with only about one-fourth of its theoretical strength; this number was further reduced to 313 when the 11th MEU was detached.*

One day after leaving the Persian Gulf, the amphibious task force received an order instructing it to prepare for possible participation in relief operations in Bangladesh. On 11 May, the Seventh Fleet ordered the ships of the amphibious task group to the Bay of Bengal to support humanitarian operations with the mission of delivering relief supplies and providing other assistance as needed. The amphibious task force was not deploying to establish a foothold, so Admiral Clarey and General Rowe expected to be in-country only a short time. The plan of action, as described by one 5th MEB staff officer, was to "hurry up, hurry in, and hurry out."[92]

Of major concern to both Admiral Clarey and General Rowe was how the weather, terrain, and hydrography of the affected region might impact operations. Additional issues were the threat of infectious diseases, the status of the refugees, the condition of lines of communication, and the ability of the Bangladesh government to cope with these problems. Both felt that relief operations were going to make heavy demands on their available communications, transportation, and medical assets.[93]

The four-day period from 11 May, when the execute order was received, to 15 May, when the amphibious task force made landfall, was devoted to planning, although the exact concept of support was unknown pending a reconnaissance of the area and coordination with the JTF staff. Despite the lack of hard information, preparations continued. The 5th MEB intelligence section prepared map studies and gave orientation lectures. The operations section worked out task organizations and prepared contingency operations plans. The logistics section reconfigured landing craft loads to carry engineer equipment and relief supplies instead of combat equipment. Helicopter crews labored to prepare desert operations-configured aircraft for the vastly different Bangladesh environment. Embarkation teams unloaded tactical equipment and supplies and reloaded engineer equipment, rations, medical supplies, and relief aid.[94]

Planning by medical personnel encompassed an analysis of medical civic action program (MedCAP) capabilities. Fifteen authorized medical allowance

---

* A Marine brigade service support group's normal strength was approximately 2,900.

blocks--five battalion aid station equipment blocks, five blocks consisting of battalion aid station consumables, and five military sick call blocks--were on hand. These supply blocks were configured for combat operations and designed to treat combat casualties, and were not intended to support disaster relief operations involving a large number of women and children. If medical civic action teams were to be deployed, it was apparent that most of their medical supplies would have to come from the Government of Bangladesh or non-government relief agencies.

Of immediate concern to amphibious task force medical personnel were the preventive measures that needed to be taken prior to beginning operations ashore. Important among these were malaria prophylaxis and immunizations for hepatitis A and typhoid. The task force possessed an outdated disease risk assessment that simply advised that the country suffered from poor sanitation and sanitary practices, so a new assessment was requested from Navy Environmental and Preventive Medicine Unit 6 outlining the malaria chemo-prophylaxis recommendations for Chittagong and outlying islands. In its response, NEMPU 6 suggested that personnel going ashore take Doxycycline for two days prior to exposure through the 28th day following the exposure. Bed and head nets, insecticides, and gamma globulin inoculations were considered essential. The unit also advised typhoid vaccinations be updated, but recommended that Marines and sailors not be immunized against cholera. Based on the unit's suggestions, all personnel going ashore were immunized against hepatitis A, typhoid, yellow fever, and started on a malaria chemo-prophylaxis. To avoid contracting cholera, they were instructed to steer clear of the local food and water supplies.[*]

As the task group neared the Bay of Bengal, PhibGru 3 and 5th MEB planners recommended the early launch of the Marine Aircraft Group's four RH-53D Sea Stallions across Indian territory to Bangladesh so that they could be available early in the relief effort. Task force planners soon scrapped the proposal because of the distance involved and the lack of maintenance support facilities along the proposed route.[95][**] Steaming around the tip of India and into position in the Bay of Bengal, one of the *Tarawa*'s embarked AV-8B

---

[*] Arrival off Bangladesh revealed that the updated disease risk assessment was based on generalizations about the country and overstated the threat of disease in and around Chittagong. Fortunately, the cyclone initially had reduced the mosquito vector population. Had the operation continued much longer, the forces ashore would have encountered a greater risk of contracting malaria.

[**] It was noted at the time and later that had the MV-22 tilt-rotor medium lift aircraft been available, "relief aircraft could have arrived on scene and begun relief operations some five days before the amphibious task force was in position to launch conventional helicopters." In addition, the transit time between the central distribution point at Chittagong and delivery landing zones could have been reduced resulting in the delivery of more relief supplies in less time. (BGen Randall L. West, Comments on draft ms, 10Apr95; MAG-50 MCLLS Report 60534-18689 (05631))

Harriers was lost while conducting deck landing qualifications on the *Vancouver*.[96]

Shortly after the amphibious task group arrived off the Bangladesh coast on the afternoon of the 15th, Admiral Clarey, General Rowe, Colonels Gangle and West, and key staff members flew to Chittagong to meet with General Stackpole. In his briefing, Stackpole outlined the situation as he saw it. There were plenty of relief supplies on shore and more were on the way. A dedicated, but inexperienced, democratic government was struggling to take control of the situation. Non-government relief agencies lacked adequate communications and transportation. During the storm, he explained, Bangladesh had lost eight ships, more than 60 percent of its helicopters, most of its fixed-wing air transport, and almost all of its communications resources. The airfield at Chittagong, at first under three feet of water, was just now being placed into operation. Most of the port's docks and piers had been carried away by the high winds and heavy surf. Inland, the major lines of communication, consisting mostly of unpaved roads and trails, had been either destroyed or rendered impassible. The massive loss of the area's livestock, a primary form of transit, seriously degraded the ability to move heavy and large items. As a result of the devastation, the most critical immediate issue was the distribution of prestaged relief supplies. Helicopters, landing craft, small boats, and ground transportation assets were needed to move food, water, medicine, and relief personnel to the remote areas devastated by the cyclone.[97]

With these issues in mind, General Stackpole told Clarey and Rowe that the

Photograph courtesy of 5th MEB

Marine BGen Peter J. Rowe, left, and RAdm Stephen S. Clarey, USN, welcome a Bangladeshi delegation on board the Tarawa.

role of PhibGru 3 and the 5th MEB was going to be delivery of the food, medicine, and expertise. The commander of the JTF assumed operational control of the amphibious task force, rather than it being placed "in support of" the JTF. General Stackpole's intent was that the Marines and sailors would be the providers, while the Bangladeshi were the implementers.

Since the amphibious task force possessed more than 90 percent of the available helicopter transport, General Stackpole assigned it the largest segment of the disaster zone. Encompassing 23,000 square kilometers, this sector included more than 240 kilometers of coastline from Chittagong in the north to Cox's Bazar in the south and the off-shore islands of South Hatia, Sandwip, Kutubdia, Manpura, and Maheshkali. Stackpole's initial plan had called for the Marine forces to be assigned to the southern sector and naval forces to the island sector. This division of labor was discussed and debated at the meeting. Both Brigadier General Rowe and Admiral Clarey, noting that a synergistic relationship had developed among the units under their command as they had been operating together for some time, recommended to General Stackpole that the JTF "capitalize on what we brought as a combined Navy/Marine Corps team."[98]   Agreeing with Rowe and Clarey, Stackpole decided that the amphibious task force should continue to operate as a single unit, thus exploiting its unique combined capabilities.

The mission assigned the amphibious task force was to provide support for relief operations to assist the government of Bangladesh; to be prepared to lift relief supplies using its landing craft and helicopter assets; and to provide medical assistance, water production, engineer and material handling equipment, security, rations, communications, and other support on short notice. General Stackpole's intent was that the mission be accomplished within two weeks, that the forces ashore, except for those guarding cryptographic materials, carry no weapons as they would not be working in a hostile environment, and that a minimum "footprint" be created by using as few Americans on shore as possible. Naval logistics support, therefore, would be sea-based throughout the operation. Helicopters would distribute relief supplies from Chittagong to the outlying areas and be refueled at sea. Marine aircraft group representatives stationed ashore would monitor, control, and dispatch aircraft for mission assignments. RLT 5 would provide material handling teams to help load, unload, and distribute relief supplies. BSSG 5 would furnish engineer support, including water production, heavy equipment and operators, and medical assistance. The ships of PhibGru 3 were to provide surface landing craft and air traffic control personnel.

The requirement for a small "footprint" ashore necessitated that there would never be more than 500 Marines, sailors, airmen, or soldiers on shore during daylight hours. Maintaining a larger force ashore would have placed an undue burden on the already beleaguered local infrastructure by increasing the demand for berthing space, sanitation facilities, and waste disposal. Logistically, requirements for food, water, and living supplies would likewise rise. Increasing the forces ashore also would mean that more Marines and sailors would risk being exposed to disease. While not a primary consideration, General Stackpole

Department of Defense Photo (USA) DA-SC-88-00434

The Tarawa *was forced to remain more than 80 kilometers off the Bangladesh coast because of strong tidal currents and contrary wind conditions.*

was aware of criticism leveled against the government by opposition parties and politicians in both Bangladesh and India. He felt that by adding more troops to the relief effort he might have added credence to their charges that American forces had been sent to Bangladesh to establish a foreign military presence in the area.[99]*

The hydrography of the Bay of Bengal dictated that the amphibious task group should be divided to support operational plans. The flagship *Tarawa* with MAG-50 embarked remained in navigable waters in a modified offshore deployment location more than 80 kilometers from Chittagong. Strong tidal currents that were generally out of phase with the prevailing winds making flight operations at anchor impossible, forced the *Tarawa* to remain underway throughout the operation.[100] The landing and transport ships moved closer to shore to facilitate material offloading by landing craft and helicopter and served as forward refueling and replenishment stations. Choppy water, tricky currents, underwater hazards, and high winds obviated operations after dark.

Since the 5th MEB would carry the major burden of the amphibious task force's relief effort, General Rowe and his staff developed a six-phase concept of operations: (1) a forward command element would be collocated with JTF Forward headquarters at Chittagong; (2) helicopter insertion of communications personnel and liaison teams into designated landing zones to coordinate operations with the JTF and relief agencies on the scene and positioning amphibious task force ships in the northern Bay of Bengal to provide sea-based logistics support; (3) lifting supplies ashore employing the brigade's helicopters and the task group's landing craft, including the movement of water-making

---

* India's West Bengal's ruling Communist Party expressed surprise over the arrival of "thousands of American" soldiers and implied that the Government of Bangladesh had handed direct responsibility for the relief effort to the Americans and suggested that U.S. forces had no intention of leaving the country "very soon." It linked the arrival of American forces to imperialist activities in west and south Asia, including alleged assistance to separatist forces in India.

facilities and potable water; (4) provide additional support as directed; (5) turn over the relief mission to international agencies or follow-on relief organizations within two weeks; and (6) backload equipment and personnel to the ships of the amphibious task force.[101]

Admiral Clarey and General Rowe, while retaining their respective posts in the amphibious task force, were designated the operation's Naval Forces and Marine Forces component commanders. As both officers now held two commands, it was necessary to appoint a mission commander to direct operations ashore personally. In making his choice, General Rowe weighed a number of competing factors. Since the mission essentially was logistical in nature, the logical choice was the commanding officer of the BSSG 5, but it was commanded by a major and General Rowe felt his rank relative to the other members of the JTF staff "could prove a hindrance, notwithstanding Major Johnson's exemplary competence." The mission commander would have to educate a joint staff that had been only recently created from diverse organizations and as yet possessed no clear understanding of command relationships or the capabilities of the amphibious task force. He would also have to secure mission orders and obtain enough latitude to accomplish the assigned tasks.

Because a major contribution to the relief effort would be helicopter transport, General Rowe's next logical choice was MAG-50's commanding officer. While Colonel West was sufficiently senior to operate within the JTF command structure, the intensity of air operations would require his undivided attention. If he was saddled with overall command of the operation ashore, MAG-50's assets might be spread too thin. Colonel Randolph Gangle was experienced in commanding a regimental landing team composed of three infantry battalions and attached artillery, tank, light armored infantry, engineer, and reconnaissance units. "Senior and savvy," he and his regimental landing team staff "were a sound base around which to form an integrated mission command."[102] "There were no book solutions to the situation," Brigadier General Rowe later noted, "it was the decision I agonized over most and it went the right way."[103]

Early on the morning of 16 May, Colonel Gangle established a mission liaison detachment in the JTF Forward headquarters at Chittagong. This detachment contained Marine and Navy personnel, including the mission commander, a Navy commander to supervise surface craft operations, the regimental landing team's operations and intelligence officers to coordinate operations, and aviation officers to create air tasking orders and coordinate aircraft control. Administrative supplies and equipment, camp provisions, communications gear, limited rolling stock, material handling equipment, ROWPUs, and other essential items also were landed at Chittagong.

Colonel Gangle's integrated staff streamlined coordination among the aviation, seaborne, and ground elements, ensuring the efficient exploitation of the amphibious task force's capabilities. Middlemen were eliminated. Gangle could, for example, speak directly with Navy Commander Thomas J. Hirsch regarding surface craft operations or to Navy air traffic control personnel without going

Photograph courtesy of Col Kevin M. Kennedy, USMC (Ret)

Mission commander, Col Randolph A. Gangle, USMC, center, coordinates relief efforts with Bangladeshi navy Capt Anwar Haque, left, and LtCol Kevin M. Kennedy, USMC, commanding officer of 2d Battalion, 5th Marines, at the Chittagong forward headquarters.

through a multi-tiered chain of command. The MAG-50 representative reported directly to the mission commander as did representatives of the service support group and regimental landing team. Colonel West, who served as air mission commander, provided Gangle with technical advice in addition to tutoring members of the JTF staff as to the most effective ways of employing scarce helicopter resources.

By 1400, Colonel Gangle's staff was established and working within the JTF's operations center. The group's functions included manning the center around the clock, coordinating with host-country personnel and civilian workers, acting as a clearing house for information, tracking operations and evaluating their effectiveness, planning future operations, networking administrative and tactical radio traffic, handling public affairs, and escorting a myriad of important visitors. While these were typical command functions, they had to be adapted for non-combat humanitarian relief operations.

In addition to Colonel Gangle's staff, the Chittagong operations center included members of the JTF Forward detachment, Bangladesh government and military personnel, American embassy staff, and representatives of several non-government relief organizations. Although this centralized location provided for enhanced coordination and cooperation, smooth working relationships among the various participants took time to develop. Disagreements arose over the number of relief centers to be established, the use and location of ROWPUs, and movement of inappropriate relief supplies. Many of the non-government organizations, such as CARE and the Red Crescent Society, had provided relief in Bangladesh for years and were accustomed to operating in their own ways, and all vied for a "piece of the action." Initially, American military and embassy personnel spent a considerable amount of time achieving a consensus among the competing organizations, training them in how to plan and organize a massive relief effort, and at the same time educating them as to the capabilities of the JTF.[104] In addition, because their logistical resources were more limited than those available to the JTF, task force and Marine brigade staff members found they needed to prod the non-government organizations to think on a grander scale--moving hundreds of tons of supplies per day instead of only 20 or 30. Mutual trust in each participant's competence and integrity, critical to the relief effort's success, developed among the various parties in the Chittagong center as all discovered a common goal.

Angels from the Sea

The amphibious task force's tactical-logistical group was in full operation on the 16th. Initial relief efforts began when MAG-50's helicopters moved 259 passengers and delivered more than 89,000 pounds of relief supplies. The operational pattern established that first day remained in effect throughout the remainder of the task force's stay.

The movement and distribution chain began with non-government organizations submitting their distribution requirements to the Bangladesh government to ensure that the requirements were compatible with the government's overall relief plan. Each morning representatives from various government ministries and non-government organizations passed a list of the following day's relief requirements and the projected needs for the next 48 hours to the JTF in Dhaka. By early afternoon, the JTF staff would publish the following day's distribution schedule, enabling suppliers time to position their cargoes at the designated loading sites for airlift from Dhaka to Chittagong and elsewhere.

The following morning, local workmen stacked relief supplies, which in turn were loaded on board Special Forces and Air Force C-130 Hercules transports. The working conditions were primitive, wrote Air Force Lieutenant Colonel White. "We didn't have any forklifts, K-loaders, pallets, nets--you name it! We floor-loaded 150-pound sacks of rice, 200-pound bags of potatoes, medical supplies, tents, etc. We managed to fly six sorties per day with only the aircrews to upload and download 40,000 pounds of cargo per sortie." Aircrews and support personnel from the 374th Tactical Airlift Wing worked from 0400 to 2000 each day until additional help in the form of loadmasters arrived from the 8th Mobile Aerial Port Squadron stationed at Clark Air Base.[105]

At Chittagong, each day began with a similar "requirements meeting." At 0730 representatives from the brigade liaison team, regimental landing team, aircraft group, amphibious task group, and Army and Air Force components met with members of the JTF staff, Bangladesh government, and the various non-

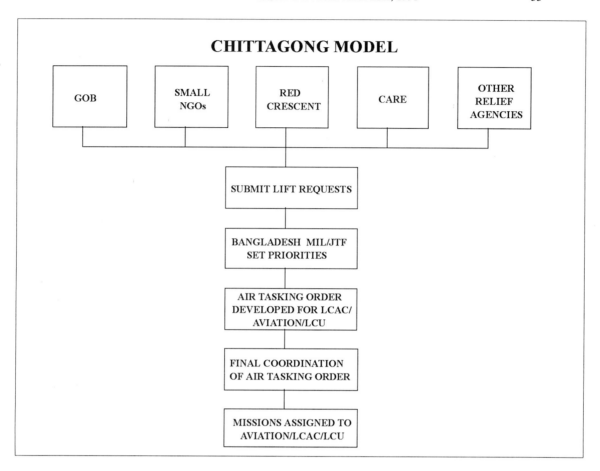

An Air Force C-130 Hercules off-loads relief supplies from Dhaka at Chittagong for further transport by air, sea, and ground to the cyclone victims.

Photograph courtesy of 5th MEB

government relief organizations to review the surface and air movement schedule for the day and determine whether there was a requirement for emergency lifts. When necessary, appropriate changes were made to the day's schedule.

The Chittagong coordinating cell scrutinized and then validated lift requirements for the following three days. Each government or non-government agency submitted its transport requirements for relief supplies, building materials, or personnel to the cell for validation. Once approved, the cell forwarded requests to the JTF operations section. This data was used to develop the daily air and surface movement schedule. The operations section would then match transportation requirements against available assets, either surface or air, based on the priority of the items, bulk, and destination. By 1600 each day, the JTF Forward staff provided each agency an air and surface schedule indicating arrival time, ramp location, quantity and type, and destination of the relief supplies. As happens in all disaster relief operations, the Marine and Army air contingents experienced a substantial number of rapid response requirements, schedule changes, and aircraft diversions during the first few days of the operation. These complications, however, diminished with time as each of the various parties gained experience in working together.[106]

As mission commander, Colonel Gangle was responsible for the air and sea movement of relief supplies, carefully balancing centralized control and decentralized effectiveness. Centralized control of mission assignments normally allowed for the efficient and orderly execution of a mission, but the Bangladesh relief effort was not a normal mission. Employing air and sea assets in support of the JTF, Bangladesh government, and non-government organizations--three sometimes competing entities--required adaptability. On the other hand, the potential for confusion and disarray existed if any one of the three organizations or staff agencies within the Chittagong operations center was given tasking control. With this in mind, Gangle based the allocation of distribution missions among helicopters and boats on load size, delivery location, and time available. Boats could serve only Sandwip, Kutubdia, and Maheshkali Islands; large, heavy loads were suited to surface lift, an optimum LCAC load was 40 to 50 tons, and an LCU could carry up to 170 tons; and time-sensitive items, such as food and medical supplies, would be sent by helicopter. He also took into consideration the relative availability of the two different means of transport.

Colonel West coordinated movement of Marine aircraft in accord with the wishes of the JTF staff and the mission commander. To do this, MAG-50 sent a forward control element ashore. The element was composed of an operations and a logistics section and a team from Navy Tactical Air Control Squadron 11 (TACRON-11). Colonel Gangle wisely allowed the Marine aircraft group staff maximum latitude to accomplish its tasks, and Colonel West felt this was a key ingredient in successfully accomplishing the mission assigned to the group.[107]

The operations section, located in the JTF operations center at the north end of Chittagong Airport, coordinated assigned aircraft to accomplish the day's missions. Each afternoon, the JTF announced its taskings for the following day. Using a dedicated satellite communications link with the flagship, the operations

Photograph courtesy of 5th MEB

The 5th MEB maintained a small command group ashore to control the flow of relief supplies.

section obtained from the tactical air control center afloat what aircraft would be available the next day. The tactical air control center on board the *Tarawa* scheduled, controlled, and monitored flights from ship to shore each morning and from shore to ship each evening. The fluid situation required maximum flexibility, so specific missions were not assigned until aircraft were actually airborne and on their way to the airfield at Chittagong. Aircraft were given new missions each time they returned to the airfield, instead of using scarce helicopter assets on multiple missions for prolonged periods that might require lengthy loiter time. In addition, missions were numbered and scheduled in order of priority, then assigned depending upon what aircraft were available during the day, therefore minimizing the disruptive impact of cancellations, change of priorities, bad weather, and mechanical problems. Flight paths and refueling times and places were left to the discretion of flight leaders and individual pilots. *Frederick* and *Barbour County*, the two amphibious tank landing ships anchored in shallow water 16 kilometers off Chittagong, served as refueling platforms. The two ships freed the aircraft from any dependence upon shore-based supplies while maintaining rapid turnaround times. A major responsibility of the operations section was to ensure all helicopters were released from their taskings in time to return to the *Tarawa* by their appointed recovery time.

The logistics section oversaw the activities of the arrival and departure airfield control groups which occupied the southern portion of the airfield from which the Marine helicopters operated. Effective communications between the operations and logistics sections kept the control groups, staffed by aircraft group logistics personnel, apprised of each inbound aircraft's assigned mission. This link also served as a backup communications system. The arrival and departure control groups also tightly managed the inventory of relief supplies, informing the JTF through the operations section of the need for replenishment. The two groups had to maintain sufficient quantities of relief supplies on hand to load all aircraft, while ensuring that no supplies remained in the groups' areas when flight operations ended each day. Any supplies left behind would be lost, either to rain damage or pilferage.

A detachment from Tactical Air Control Squadron 11 augmented the Marine aviation element. The TACRON staff provided several key functions. After initial difficulties communicating with the tower, the squadron supplied a qualified air traffic controller equipped with a ultra-high frequency (UHF) radio to Chittagong airfield. This was critical because MAG-50's UH-1N helicopters were not equipped with very-high frequency, amplitude modulation, VHF (AM) radios, the only type of radio used by the tower.* It was also reassuring to have an English-speaking controller to work out language difficulties. He recorded 11 "saves" in an equal number of days standing tower watch.[108] The control group also passed on important weather, tasking, safety, flight, and navigational information. Initially, navigation proved a problem due to the unreliability of non-directional beacons, the absence of a shore-based tactical air navigation system, and the lack of long-range navigation chain coverage. Few local maps were available, but aircrews and relief parties improvised tactical pilotage charts by photocopying and taping together the 8-1/2 by 11-inch sheets to form useful mosaics.** Although originally intended for use by ground units, helicopter aircrews made use of the few available small, lightweight global positioning system receivers.

One of the 5th MEB's major contributions to the JTF was to augment it with the brigade's command element and service support group. Although equipment and logistics expertise was important, the most important support provided was communications. Neither the Bangladesh government nor the relief agencies had sufficient communications resources, due either to a lack of equipment or because existing equipment had been damaged or destroyed. As a result, Bangladesh government officials and military officers were unable to communicate with each other or with their units and offices in the disaster zone. Fifteen hundred non-government volunteer workers had come to Bangladesh, but their agencies could not transport them to the field or communicate with representatives already there.

---

* Prior to the arrival of the air traffic controller, HMLA-169 made an attempt to assign discrete ultra-high frequencies for the Chittagong tower, but the attempt proved futile as tower workers refused to monitor the UHF net. The refusal resulted in the squadron's UH-1Ns using the UHF guard normally assigned to aircraft with emergency problems. In addition, the squadron attempted to fly multi-plane formations with the lead aircraft equipped with one of two available ARC-182s, a radio providing VHF (AM), VHF (FM), and UHF (AM) capabilities within the same unit. This solution worked well until the squadron's aircraft were forced to operate separately for most missions.

** While enroute, the amphibious task group requested the appropriate support maps through CinCPacFlt and CinCPac from the Defense Mapping Agency. A partial fill of the order was received on 25 May, four days before the amphibious task force was to cease operations.

The Joint Task Force also experienced similar problems as promised supplemental communications personnel and equipment had not arrived.

The JTF's primary concern was a central command net tying together the JTF, CinCPac, and III MEF. It fell to the brigade's communications officer, Lieutenant Colonel William V. Cantu, and a detachment from the 5th SRISG to develop a communications plan and establish a communications net covering all aspects of air, ground, and seaborne operations. The net consisted of 10 to 12 communications sites using assets from the JTF, the 5th MEB, and flown-in equipment of the 7th Communications Battalion. Small detachments, each consisting of only two or three Marines, manned high-frequency radios at key government buildings, relief storehouses, and distribution points. These sites supported Bangladesh government and non-government relief agencies. Although only a temporary measure, the communications detachments doubled the amount of supplies reaching the Chittagong distribution center. Relying on Marine communications, the government was able to coordinate relief efforts and simultaneously rebuild its damaged commercial communications links to the disaster zone. Despite the very austere living conditions, reported Lieutenant Colonel Kevin M. Kennedy, commanding officer of Battalion Landing Team 2/5, "the teams really enjoyed the assignment."[109]

Full-scale relief operations began on the morning of 17 May. The first day of operations set a pattern that remained in place throughout the operation. At first light, helicopters and landing craft carried personnel and equipment ashore. After unloading, personnel and transportation assets were directed to one of the five distribution points. As Air Force and Special Forces C-130s arrived at the designated C-130 ramp at Chittagong's Patenga Airport, regimental landing team forklifts off-loaded the cargo. The cargo and the considerable amount of relief supplies stockpiled at the airport by government and non-government agencies then were moved to the initial loading points: the northern ramp, from which the five Army UH-60 Blackhawk helicopters operated; the south ramp, where Marine RH-53 Sea Stallions and CH-46 Sea Knights were stationed; or the "J" ramp used by two Aerospatiale AS 365N Dauphin emergency medical service helicopters and a 50-man Japanese relief team. The amphibious task group located its LCAC ramp at the fuel jetty off the Karnaphuli River. The LCU ramp, located at the port's ferry landing, was used by utility landing craft. A ramp director controlled each loading site and organized the activities of the ramp in accordance with the daily mission schedule. At the end of the day, each director reported to the JTF the amount of relief supplies moved.

Once the relief supplies had been moved to their designated ramp, brigade material handling teams took over, loading the aircraft and unloading them at landing zones scattered throughout southeastern Bangladesh. Bangladesh civilian laborers loaded and unloaded the surface craft. The Americans provided muscle and lift assets, but they did not interfere with delivery priority or selection of distribution locations. When these missions were completed or as darkness fell, the handling teams on shore were picked up and returned to their respective ships.

Department of Defense Photo (USAF) DF-ST-92-06120
A Marine CH-46 Sea Knight helicopter lands as an Air Force 374th Tractical Air Wing C-130 Hercules prepares for take-off at Chittagong airfield.

Tracking the wide variety of missions spread across a 23,000-square kilometer area of operations was difficult. Close liaison between JTF, government representatives, and non-government relief workers was crucial if supplies were to reach those who most needed them. Careful planning was required to ensure the proper tools were being used, that supplies were being delivered where they were most needed, and to avoid redundant or useless missions. For aircraft this was accomplished by creating an air tasking order that matched available aircraft and their capabilities with mission needs. Navy representatives used similar schedules to plan landing craft missions.

The mission control centers resembled combat operations centers familiar to all Marines. Busy watch officers manned a bank of phones, scribbled messages, and answered questions. Area maps were dotted with colored pins and colored markers that showed unit locations. Constant updating of this information was imperative to keep decision makers abreast of the fluid situation and ever-changing requirements. Charts detailed air and surface craft missions, noting the scheduled time, date, location, delivery area, and load configuration--passengers, weight, or items. Other charts and maps indicated current status of assets, delivery priorities, planned routes, call signs and radio frequencies, alternate plans, escape and evasion routes, and rally points.

The distribution teams were manned primarily by the 5th Marines Surveillance and Target Acquisition Platoon, officers from the ground combat element, and other specialists as needed. These small detachments moved into the disaster area to replace or reinforce Special Forces disaster relief teams already in place. By doing this, the 5th MEB was able to triple the number of

Department of Defense Photo (USAF) DF-ST-92-02634

Air Force, Marine and Army personnel coordinate supply deliveries from a communications site at Chittagong airfield.

receiving points in the hardest-hit areas. Once in place, they coordinated resupply efforts, radioed situation reports to the command center, and provided terminal guidance at the landing zones. Distribution points usually were manned by American or Bangladesh military personnel, a few relief workers, and at least one government representative. Marine engineers often set up water purification units at these sites, which also soon became favorite places to establish medical treatment centers.

Surface craft carried a large portion of the relief aid that was moved during the operation. They included LCACs, LCUs, rigid raiding craft, and inflatable boats.* The nature of the operations area made these craft ideal for distribution missions, however, the forces of nature put excellent seamanship at a premium. Winds reached velocities of up to 50 knots, there was a 12-foot tidal rise, and ever-shifting 12-knot currents swirled between the islands and the mainland.[110]

The Chittagong headquarters established landing beaches on Sandwip, Manpura, Kutubdia, Matabari, and Maheshkali Islands. Air-cushion landing craft soon became the stars of the show. The image of LCACs rushing over the water, kicking up a silvery spray as they made their runs to the shore while

---

* Commander Thomas J. Hirsch quickly determined that the amphibious task group's LCM-8s were unsuitable for the relief effort as they were not self-sustaining for personnel. They remained on board the *Tarawa* well to seaward throughout Sea Angel and did not participate in the relief operation.

Photograph courtesy of 5th MEB
An air-cushion landing craft being loaded with relief supplies for transport to one of the the offshore islands.

carrying 30 to 40 tons at speeds up to 50 knots, became synonymous with the operation. Unfortunately, the LCACs were designed to carry rolling stock, not bulk cargo, so loading and unloading was less efficient than when carrying vehicles. Local delivery trucks were not transported because they lacked appropriate tie downs and were often loaded beyond axle capacity. The Bangladesh government hired laborers to load and unload the four LCACs. Military and police personnel provided security around the off-load ramps to restrain curiosity seekers who often numbered up to 10,000. The air-cushion landing craft returned to their ships each night, often carrying a load to be delivered the following morning.

Other craft provided yeoman service as well. Unlike the LCACs, the three LCUs required most of a day to load, depending upon the arrival time of the relief supplies. These boats remained overnight when loaded, delivered their cargo the next morning, and returned to their assigned ship that evening. Small rigid raiding craft manned by Navy SEALs and reconnaissance Marines proved ideal for moving supplies through the numerous waterways that crisscrossed the islands and coastal lowlands. These boats proved very useful for short hauls and their small loads were manageable for local laborers working without forklifts or motor transport.

Marine amphibious assault vehicles were launched but quickly encountered difficulties. Their top water speed was only about eight knots, so they could not be used in the face of 8- to 12-knot currents. In addition, the silt-ladened water soon fouled their propulsion systems, leaving them to drift at the mercy of the

Photograph courtesy of 5th MEB

Local laborers unload food and construction materials from one of the three LCUs used during the relief operation.

prevailing currents and tides.* The vehicles were recovered and did not assist in the relief operation. Had the AAVs made it to shore, the treads of these 25-ton monsters would have damaged the fragile infrastructure and most probably ruptured the packed-dirt embankments that held the tides at bay.

The ships of PhibGru 3 provided splendid support throughout the operation. The "blue-green" Navy-Marine team had been improving sea-based logistics since the Vietnam War. This concept relied on ships of the fleet for combat service support rather than building logistics bases ashore. Sea-basing the 5th MEB had been pioneered by General Rowe's predecessor, Brigadier General William P. Eshelman. General Rowe refined the concept and used it to the fullest during the recent deployment to the Persian Gulf. The result was that PhibGru 3 and the 5th MEB were very familiar with the concept and implemented it easily in the Bay of Bengal.

One visible example of sea-basing was the use of the LSTs *Barbour County* and *Frederick* for aviation support. Both ships broke away from the task group and moved close to shore in order to facilitate the unloading of supplies. During the operation, they remained at anchor in less than 10 meters of water where they could act as forward replenishment platforms. A friendly rivalry between the two ships soon emerged when they vied to see which could service the most

---

* The three LCUs encountered similar problems with the silt-laden water, but with constant maintenance remained able to perform their assigned relief missions.

aircraft. Arriving helicopters were quickly refueled and their crews were given box lunches and cold sodas. Using the acronym "BoB" for Bay of Bengal, the *Barbour County* was soon tabbed "BoB's Service Station." The deck crew outfitted a cork mannequin with a cranial helmet, goggles, flotation vest, steel-toed boots, and work suit to play the role of friendly "Bob," the station manager. "Bob's arm was raised in a constant gesture of warm welcome or fond farewell, depending on whether your were landing or taking off." The *Barbour County* even offered free ship's baseball caps to the 100th customer in a spoof of American service station marketing strategies.[111]

The general daily aviation plan was to use the Blackhawks, Sea Knights, and Sea Stallions, and the two Japanese Dauphin helicopters, to deliver working parties and move bulk cargo, such as large bags of rice, potatoes, lentils, dry molasses, flour, and wheat. They also carried Bangladesh officials, non-government relief workers, medical teams, water purification units, livestock, VIPs, and members of the media.[112*] The preferred delivery method was to sling-load cargo whereby an entire load could be hooked up or dropped off in minutes, instead of the hours it might take to load and unload using stevedore labor. The main drawback to this method was that safe operating procedures dictated slings could not be used when helicopters were carrying passengers.

Colonel West used the aircraft group's light helicopters to deliver small loads directly to the disaster area, notably to the islets just off the north coast of Sandwip Island. Hueys, flown by skilled pilots, set down at minuscule landing zones such as roof tops or paddy dikes to deliver loads of up to 1,500 pounds. Bags of rice and lentils were emptied in minutes by hungry Bangladeshis who quickly got in line for their cup or double handful. Colonel West reported that on one such mission he saw the village chief clasping his hands together and nodding with tears in his eyes to acknowledge the first food and fresh water delivery since the cyclone struck. In a note later passed to West, the grateful village chief explained that a baby born that day had been named Faresta. It was done, he said, to serve as a reminder to the village of the *faresta*, or angels, sent by their American friends in their time of great need.[113] "The words 'faresta, faresta, . . .' became frequently heard shouts from smiling and waving villagers as helos came in and out of landing zones, delivering badly needed food, water, and medical supplies."[114]

Ironically, the major supply problem was that there was too much on hand. Humanitarian relief was flooding into Bangladesh, but it could not be moved to the forward areas. This was particularly true for items too big or too delicate to be manhandled by Bangladeshi workers. Non-government relief workers and

---

* Early in the operation, CinCPac authorized the Joint Task Force to transport foreign nationals and members of the news media on American military aircraft. Initially, flight requests from the media came with little or no warning, and inadequate consolidation. However, with careful management, maximum use was made of every helicopter. When transporting the press or VIPs, any extra space was filled with rice or other relief supplies.

Photograph courtesy of 5th MEB

A Marine CH-46 Sea Knight helicopter is besieged by starving villagers as it delivers food and medical supplies to an outlying village.

government officials understood the problem, but were helpless to do much because they lacked the proper equipment; therefore, the assets the amphibious task force brought to Bangladesh became crucial to the operation's success.

Almost every Marine volunteered to go ashore, but not all could be sent at one time, so General Rowe instituted a rotation system to allow as many Marines as possible to get ashore and see what Operation Productive Effort was all about. Working parties of 50 to 100 Marines were organized every day to help move relief materials. The Americans and Bangladeshis soon were working side by side and from all outward signs, they worked together with efficiency, team spirit, and camaraderie. The sight of a robust Marine throwing a 50-pound sack of rice around with ease quickly awed the Bangladeshis. The ultimate status symbol for a Bangladeshi was to be invited on board one of the helicopters, and they soon began mirroring the American "bucket brigade" method of passing bags of food, building materials, and medical supplies from person to person. Within a few days it was common practice for the Bangladeshis to give the Marines a broad smile and a distinctive "thumbs up" sign when the work day ended.*

As the relief effort moved into high gear on the 17th, General Stackpole and his planning section in Dhaka made a number of final refinements and then

---

* For many Bangladeshis, the "thumbs up" sign is an obscene gesture. Obviously, this cultural prejudice temporarily faded with Operation Sea Angel.

Department of Defense Photo (USAF) DF-ST-92-02649

A common sight at numerous villages throughout southeastern Bangladesh was a Marine hurrying to unload sacks of rice and potatoes.

submitted the task force's completed campaign plan to CinCPac for approval. The plan was based on four assumptions: first, duration of the operation was approximately 30 days; second, the Government of Bangladesh would want the JTF to remain for the duration; third, the amphibious task group was to depart on 29 May; and fourth, the *St. Louis* and Marine Contingency Air-Group Task Force 2-91 would arrive on 29 May. The goal was to stabilize the situation in Bangladesh, allowing the government to assume full responsibility for long-term recovery, assisted by normal American foreign aid. The restoration of the infrastructure within the disaster region was to be the government's main focus, while the JTF would concentrate on assisting Bangladesh in stabilizing the situation until the country could recover from the initial effects of the cyclone and begin its own rebuilding program.

The campaign plan, as envisioned, encompassed three phases. The first was to "conduct humanitarian operations designed to immediately reduce mortality and stabilize the situation to begin recovery operations." The primary focus of the first phase would be on distribution. This phase was scheduled to last approximately 14 days. During phase two, the efforts of the JTF would be directed toward the delivery of supplies and equipment that would allow the residents of the affected areas to begin self-help recovery projects. General Stackpole estimated that phase two would require approximately 10 days to complete. In the final phase, which he estimated would take five days, the Bangladesh government would assume full control of the relief effort. The JTF would continue to provide technical advice and humanitarian assistance, and then withdraw. Pacific Command quickly approved the plan.[115]

General Stackpole realized that the transition from one phase to another would not be clear-cut and would vary from one area to another. To avoid offending local sensitivities, American forces would not be involved in the disposal of human or animal remains. Likewise, American and subordinate commanders were not to engage in open-ended activities or long-term projects that would go beyond the JTF's original charter of conducting life-sustaining operations. "We could not do that," Stackpole later noted, "nor did we have the heavy equipment" to rebuild embankments, clear more than 20 wrecks from the Karnaphuli River, restore power, or repair microwave communications towers. "We were not staying there forever," a point which General Stackpole continually stressed and which permeated all planning from the very beginning.[116]

At first, relief efforts were limited to the vicinity of Chittagong, however, operations rapidly expanded and soon included many outlying areas and offshore islands. On 19 May, Colonel Gangle ordered Lieutenant Colonel Donald R. Selvage, commanding officer of Battalion Landing Team 3/5, to move ashore from the *Vancouver* and to establish a second control center at Cox's Bazar, a small resort city located at the southern tip of the area of operations. Its 6,000-foot airfield and small boat harbor became the focal points for relief efforts on Kutubdia, Maheshkali, and several of the smaller islands in the vicinity.

Department of Defense Photo (USN) DN-ST-90-05402

The Vancouver *transported LtCol Donald R. Selvage's 3d Battalion, 5th Marines, south to Cox's Bazar, where a second control center was established on 19 May.*

Lieutenant Colonel Selvage followed the Chittagong model in organizing and conducting the relief activities at Cox's Bazar. The Deputy Zonal Relief Coordinator for Cox's Bazar and Deputy Commissioners for both Cox's Bazar and Naokhali districts provided Selvage's staff, located at the city's airport, with daily lift requirements. Based upon those requirements, the staff developed daily mission schedules.

Battalion Landing Team 3/5's efforts at Cox's Bazar received a welcome boost when Britain's Royal Navy and Royal Marines reported for duty with the JTF. Royal Fleet Auxiliary replenishment ship *Fort Grange* (A 385) arrived off the port city on 20 May after a short passage from Colombo in Sri Lanka.[*] The *Fort Grange* carried a 200-man crew and 20 Royal Marines from 539 Assault Squadron, four 846 Naval Air Squadron Westland HAS.5 Sea King commando medium-lift transport helicopters, six rigid raiding craft, and assorted inflatable boats.[**]

Following an air reconnaissance of the area to locate a secure operations base from which boats could operate at all tidal levels, the Royal Marines launched their relief effort on 22 May. A daily routine was established consisting of boat runs between Cox's Bazar and Dhalghata and Matabari Villages on the island of Matabari and Gorakghata Pier on Maheshkali Island. At last light, the Royal Marines flew back to the *Fort Grange*, leaving two behind to secure the base. While they enjoyed an "outstanding" working relationship with their American counterparts, they also shared a common problem--navigating an area choked

---

[*] The Royal Fleet Auxiliary is similar to the United States Military Sealift Command; both feature Navy-owned, civilian-manned, non-amphibious, combat support ships.

[**] The Westland HC.4 Sea King helicopter was the British commando assault version of the Sikorsky SH-3 Sea King helicopter used by the U.S. Navy; it could carry 28 personnel or 8,000 pounds of cargo.

with floating debris and fish traps and shifting channels and sand bars. The British soon found out that local navigational charts and maps were outdated.[117]

As Operation Productive Effort advanced it evolved from a joint, denoting inter-Service, into a combined or international, military humanitarian operation. British, Pakistani, and Japanese troops were integrated into the JTF and provided liaison personnel at Dhaka, Chittagong, and Cox's Bazar who accepted missions as assigned by the coordination cells. While the British concentrated on two major islands off Chittagong, the Japanese generally flew utility missions suited to their two small helicopters, as did the two Pakistani helicopters. The Indians and Chinese did not subordinate their helicopters to the joint effort, but did establish informal agreements with the JTF by which they would cover certain areas when allied assets could not assist or were otherwise employed.

By the second week of the massive relief operation, the effort had settled into an efficient routine. Military Airlift Command Galaxies and Starlifters arrived at Zia International bringing in water purification units from Okinawa, communications packages and personnel from the Air Force's 4th Combat Communications Group on Guam, and C-130 aircraft maintenance packages from Yokota Air Base in Japan. Air Force C-130s, Marine and Army helicopters, and Navy surface craft hauled food and medical supplies. On the ground, Marine engineers set-up water purification units and Army Special Forces relief teams provided on-site assessment.

The relief effort soon was expanded to include the Sylhet region of north-

Department of Defense Photo (USN) DF-ST-90-06106

Mrs. Marilyn T. Quayle, wife of the Vice President, greets Marines upon her arrival at Chittagong.

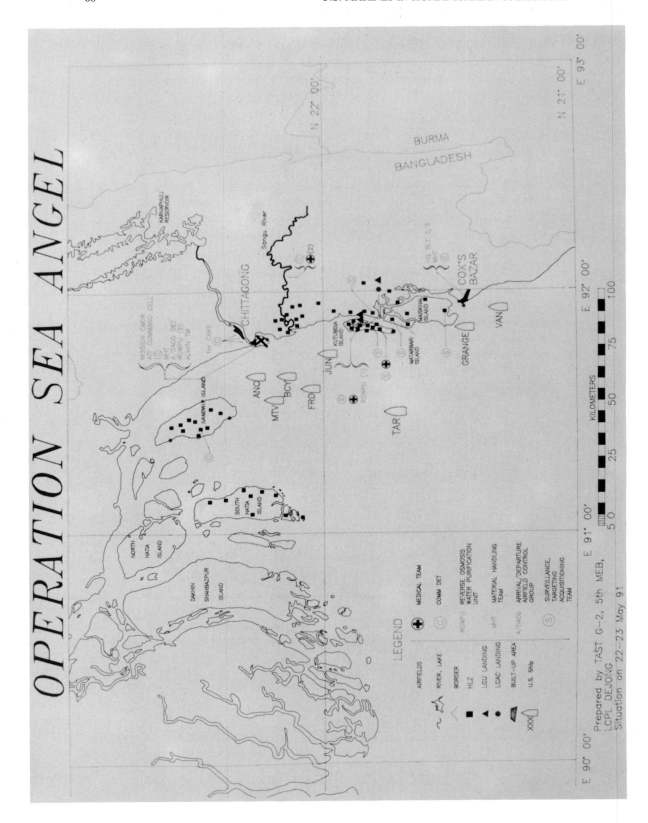

eastern Bangladesh, hard hit by monsoonal flooding. Hercules C-130 transports flew three or four daily sorties between Dhaka and the city of Sylhet, carrying more than 25 tons of supplies each day. Chinese and Indian helicopters assisted with the local distribution of these supplies. In addition, Mrs. Marilyn T. Quayle, Chairman of the American Advisory Committee for Foreign Disaster Assistance and wife of Vice President J. Danforth Quayle, visited American forces and toured the disaster area. She and her small official party remained overnight on board the flagship *Tarawa*, where security, medical, and communications facilities were available. Among other visitors were ambassadors representing the nations involved and senior members of the Bangladesh government, including President Justice Shahabuddin Ahmed and Prime Minister Zia. The week also witnessed the signing of a formal status of forces agreement between Bangladesh and the United States which accorded JTF personnel status equivalent to that provided to members of the administrative and technical staff of the American Embassy in Bangladesh. American military personnel were also granted freedom of movement, exemption from local taxation and tariff charges, and immunity from the jurisdiction of local courts.[118]

During the second week, the operation and the JTF were renamed. "Well done to all involved in ongoing relief operations for the people of Bangladesh," read the message from the Chairman of the Joint Chiefs of Staff, General Colin L. Powell. He then quoted a recent news story describing U.S. relief forces as "angels from the sea." According to Powell, the quote "carries the true spirit of our work and inspired a change to the name of our operations. Effective immediately, Operation 'Productive Effort' will be called 'Sea Angel.'"[119] As General Stackpole later commented: "it worked out extremely well because that indeed encapsulized and described the functions that we were carrying out."[120]

One of the greatest threats to the success of Operation Sea Angel was the toll taken by infectious disease. Providing food and shelter was not enough. If proper medical care and clean water were not forthcoming, more people would perish from disease than would die from starvation or as a direct result of the cyclone. A medical management team headed by Captain John R. Downs, MC, USNR, and supported by Lieutenant Colonel Craig S. Matsuda, MC, USAF, and Lieutenant Commander Pete L. Godbey, MC, USN, oversaw the Joint Task Force's medical relief effort.

Arriving in Dhaka on 14 May, the team met with the appropriate government ministers and their secretaries who had jurisdiction over health care, water, and sanitation, as well as physicians at the International Center for Diarrheal Disease Research, Bangladesh; USAID personnel; and representatives of several non-government relief organizations. All agencies involved agreed that the primary concern was to ensure an adequate supply of safe drinking water. This would require the repair of existing tubewells, the placement of additional wells, the distribution of water purifying agents, and an engineering study of tubewells, water collection ponds, and embankments by Navy Mobile Construction Battalion personnel. The second priority was to ensure an adequate food supply and then the prompt treatment of diarrheal diseases. As oral rehydration solutions were

Photograph courtesy of PhibGru 3

Col Mike Ferguson, USAF, right, chief of staff of the forward headquarters, displays the new Combined Joint Task Force banner with draftsman Regaul Karim.

in short supply, one of the JTF's major efforts would be to provide the capability for treating diarrheal outbreaks with intravenous rehydration solutions and antibiotics. Mobile medical civic action program (MedCAP) teams would be deployed throughout the affected area to provide care, and lastly, the JTF would attempt to provide temporary shelter materials, such as plastic sheeting, and then building materials to repair destroyed homes.

With the establishment of the forward headquarters at Chittagong, Captain Downs and Lieutenant Commander Godbey, who was responsible for coordinating medical operations within the disaster area, supervised the opening of a small aid station. They also met with local medical officials. At the meeting, the district's chief surgeon told the JTF medical representatives that Sandwip Island and the hard-hit subdistrict of Banshkhali, south of the city, had the highest priorities. As a result, NEPMU 6 was tasked with surveying Sandwip and Banshkhali for a team site. Sandwip Island was finally chosen by the unit as the location for its quasi-health department. From this base, the unit carried out an epidemiology, entomology, preventive medicine, and microbiological assessment of the island. While not quantifiable, the findings would assist the inhabitants of Sandwip Island prepare for disease control during and after future disasters. In addition, the unit initiated a program of disease surveillance throughout the area's remaining subdistricts. A computer database was constructed and the data collected from all affected regions was analyzed to identify areas of greatest need.[121]

Following the arrival of the amphibious task group, Captain Downs flew out to the *Tarawa* where he met PhibGru 3 and 5th MEB medical staffs. He identified a reservoir of approximately eight medical civic action program teams formed from the brigade.* Practical and political considerations weighed toward using MedCAP teams to augment and work with local medical professionals. In addition to providing assistance and education, the teams could initiate programs and procedures that could be carried on by those who permanently served the population. Treatment without continuity was of little long-term value.

The JTF surgeon designated the *Tarawa* as the primary casualty receiving and treatment ship for American forces in the Chittagong area. A small ward and a seven-bed intensive care unit were also set aside at the combined military hospital in Dhaka. A similar arrangement was made with the Chittagong Comprehensive Military Hospital. These hospitals provided sufficient emergency care to treat and stabilize any injury or disease suffered by American personnel prior to being evacuated by air.

The JTF medical management team conducted an overland assessment of Patiya, Anwara, Banshkhali, Chakaria, and Maheskhali subdistricts. They ended their tour in Cox's Bazar. Medical civic action program sites were identified and assessed by Special Operations Forces disaster relief teams which, working in concert with local Bangladeshi Special Forces units, provided medical intelligence and other support information to Captain Downs and his staff. The subdistrict survey, and meetings with local medical personnel, resulted in the definition of district priorities--the highest being Sandwip and Hatia Islands and the coastal areas of Anwara and Banshkhali. In addition, the management team established a protocol for inserting the MedCAP teams. No team would be deployed without the presence of translators and local authorities. Coordination between local authorities, the Special Forces team, and the MedCAP team at each site was stressed. And initially, the teams would work at local subdistrict hospitals.[122]

The first MedCAP team deployed to Kutubdia Island on the morning of 19 May. Later, additional teams were sent to Anwara and Patiya subdistricts and Matabari Island. By the 20th, six teams were rotating throughout the affected area. Each team consisted of a Navy doctor and four or five corpsmen. They were briefed at the Chittagong headquarters, given medical supplies, water, prepackaged meals, and background information on the selected site and surrounding area before deploying forward.

The experiences of the Kutubdia Island team typified MedCAP operations throughout the disaster area. Navy Reserve Lieutenant John E. Koella, battalion surgeon for the 2d Battalion, 11th Marines; four corpsmen; and a Reserve Marine sergeant from TOW Platoon, 23d Marines, who was a civilian nurse, arrived at the Kutubdia Health Complex from the *Anchorage* early on the 19th.

---

* The MedCAP teams were formed exclusively from 5th MEB personnel, as PhibGru 3 medical personnel had shipboard responsibilities that precluded them from going ashore.

72

The team was accompanied by a Bangladeshi medical researcher; a nurse and public health specialist from USAID, who was seconded full-time from Dhaka to assist the JTF public health effort; and a public health nurse with Project Concern.   Funded by Bangladesh, American, and other non-government agencies, the Health Complex encompassed a small outpatient clinic, a 50-bed inpatient hospital, and a regional medical administration office.   The sole permanent medical facility on the island, it served a population of more than 120,000 prior to the cyclone.[123]

The complex was surrounded by standing water, mud, and sewage.   The interior of the hospital, which held more than 80 patients, was worse, as Lieutenant Koella reported:

> There was no electricity or running water.   Potable water was obtained from a nearby tubewell.   There were no hand-held urinals, bed pans, or bedside commodes, and few actual beds for inpatients.   Most inpatients were either too weak or too ill-informed to try and use hospital toilets, and they defecated, vomited, and urinated onto the hospital floor.   In the inpatient facility the majority of patients had no bed or mattress and they rested on the floor, which was awash in diarrhea, urine, and vomitus.   There was a cloud of flies covering each patient.   Ants covered IV bags as they infused fluids, and at night mosquitoes swarmed.[124]

Lieutenant Koella's team assumed responsibility for all inpatient care from 0600 to 1800 each day, local staff managed care from 1800 to 0600.   Local physicians staffed the outpatient clinic and referred the most serious cases to the team for screening and treatment.   A constant stream of outpatients, regulated by a Bangladesh army disaster relief unit, sought the team's care after normal working hours.

The team initially augmented the local staff and Bangladesh army and navy medical relief teams.   The arrival of additional civilian medical workers from the country's Postgraduate Medical Training Hospital in Dhaka relieved the local physicians and staff of their outpatient duties, allowing them to concentrate temporarily on administrative matters and remedying the facility's sanitation problems.   Running water was restored, albeit intermittently, floors were cleaned and bleached, new mattresses obtained, and flies and ants controlled.

Inpatient admissions averaged 50 per day, with an average stay of 36 hours. Approximately 70 percent of those admitted suffered moderate to severe dehydration with watery diarrhea, assumed to be cholera, and 20 percent had abdominal cramps accompanied by bloody diarrhea, caused by the Shigella bacteria.   A majority of the remaining 10 percent had infected soft tissue injuries directly attributable to the cyclone.   The rest suffered from severe malnutrition, oral fungus infections, advanced bony and soft tissue tumors, bowel obstructions,

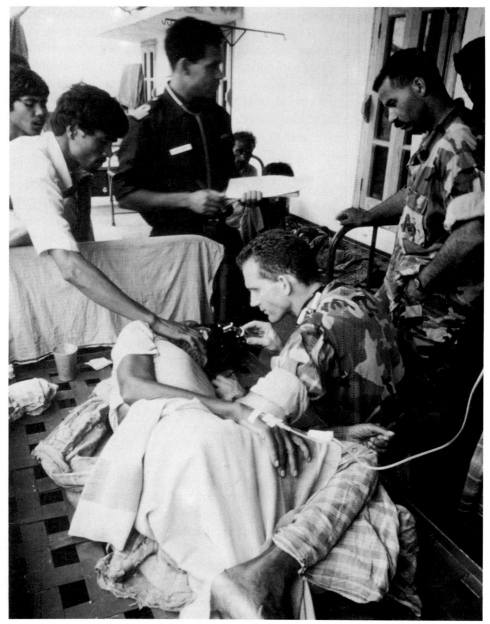

Department of Defense Photo (USAF) DF-ST-92-06131

Lt John Koella, a doctor with the 2d Battalion, 11th Marines, examines a patient at the Kutubdia Health Complex as Hospital Corpsman 1st Class Robert Andrews stands by.

persistent and intractable asthma, and eye infections. Outpatients numbered about 120 per day and generally suffered from minor or chronic orthopedic and dermatological problems.

After a five-day stay, during which the Health Complex staff was reinforced substantially by civilian physicians, Koella's team returned to the *Anchorage*.

Unfortunately, as the battalion surgeon later noted, the newly arrived physicians were not accompanied by a sufficient number of nurses or other health workers. "We did not need more doctors, we needed nurses," he reported. "Never before in my career has the importance of good nursing care been so vividly displayed." Koella continued: "Patients went unfed, uncleaned, uneducated, and uncared for; IVs ran out; meds were not passed reliably; and records were lost or mixed up. We cannot change ingrained Bengali attitudes overnight, but we must impress upon Bengali officials the need for more appreciation of the benefits of adequate nursing care."[125]

By 21 May, reports from the six medical civic action teams indicated that the patient load of diarrheal diseases was stabilized in all areas. As the amount of medical supplies and the number of non-government health professionals airlifted into the area increased, so did the volume of evacuated patients. Based on the recommendations of the MedCAP teams, patients with tetanus, abdominal obstructions caused by worms, infected traumatic wounds, and all pediatric and infected multiple fracture cases, were flown to Chittagong. The patients were then transferred to the medical school of the city's hospital where they received appropriate care. One ethnic group was excluded--Muslim Burmese who had immigrated to Bangladesh. Because they were Burmese and not Bangladeshi, government officials did not designate this hard-hit group as a priority for relief aid. To avoid a political confrontation or inflaming ethnic sensitivities, Captain Downs arranged for the *Fort Grange* to provide food, medical supplies, and care to the Burmese.

On 25 May, with the medical conditions of most areas stabilized, the MedCAP teams were withdrawn and replaced by government and non-government medical personnel. While ashore, 5th MEB corpsmen and physicians saw and treated more than 15,000 patients, and supervised the distribution of 38 metric tons of medical supplies. "Their exposure to the disease, sanitation and population problems present in Bangladesh will have an impact on [all doctors and corpsmen] for the rest of their lives," reported General Stackpole, "they will be far better health practitioners because of their exposure." In addition, "many thousands of Bangladesh citizens were directly impacted because of the health care given by our MedCAP teams."[126] The contributions of the 5th MEB and JTF medical teams were not short-lived. The impact of educational programs, such as instruction provided to local health authorities in pediatric care, and the sharing of knowledge between health and medical professionals would outlast the short-term emergency assistance provided by the MedCAP teams.

To cover the cost of medical support and the numerous other types of assistance provided by the JTF, on 26 May President Bush, with the advice of the Departments of State and Defense, authorized "the furnishing of up to $20 million of defense articles from the stocks of the Department of Defense and defense services of the Department of Defense," for Bangladesh disaster assistance.[127] This presidential determination, based on section 506 (a) (2) of the Foreign Assistance Act of 1961, as amended, would later cause some

Photograph courtesy of 5th MEB

A Marine RH-53, two CH-46s, and a UH-1N belonging to MAG-50, stage to receive relief supplies at Chittagong airfield.

confusion. Initially, it was assumed that it would cover the total cost of all JTF-provided goods such as food, medical supplies, and shelter materials, and services such as transportation, water purification, and basic engineering work. However, State Department and CinCPac legal staffs subsequently determined that it only applied to assistance provided for 120 days after the presidential determination was issued.[128]* Following the termination of Operation Sea Angel, the American Embassy, through the defense attache's office, would use this presidential determination to upgrade the Bangladesh government's disaster relief network by providing Department of Defense-declared excess equipment, such as radios and other communications gear.

As the month of May came to a close, General Stackpole realized that the three phases of the campaign were culminating at different times in different regions. It was not possible to characterize the operation as entirely into any given phase at any given time. By 27 May, however, there was a consensus that

---

* The costs associated with Operation Sea Angel eventually were funded, with the assurance of later reimbursement, by each service component from its operations and maintenance budget, with the explanation that the operation offered a "tremendous training opportunity." The costs per service were: Marine Corps, $514,000; Navy, $2,968,000; Army, $500,000; Air Force, $2,241,000; and other defense agencies, $127,000. Originally, the Department of Defense anticipated that the Department of State would reimburse the department for its disaster assistance efforts. However, it later was determined that each of the services' operations and maintenance budgets would be reimbursed with money drawn from the Defense Emergency Response Fund, established by Congress in 1990. (LtGen Henry C. Stackpole III, statement before House Armed Services Subcommittee on Readiness, 31Mar92). For a list of forms of assistance provided by the United States, see Appendix D.

all areas were stabilized and were ready for the transition back to a primarily Bangladeshi effort. Despite a decrease in donor and government relief supplies, the JTF's air and sealift campaign continued, lifting everything available and ensuring that the outlying storage and distribution facilities were stocked with the needed supplies.[129]

As the allotted two-week deployment period of the amphibious task group came to an end on the 28th, Marine Aircraft Group 50 ended helicopter operations and closed its forward air centers at Chittagong and Dhaka. In addition, Battalion Landing Team 3/5 turned over coordination of the relief effort at the Cox's Bazar distribution center to a British liaison cell from the *Fort Grange*. At about 1900, with the retrograde of personnel and equipment to the ships of the amphibious task group complete, Colonel Gangle and his liaison team departed. That evening, American officers and their Bangladeshi military counterparts got together for a small farewell party. The Bangladeshis presented each American with the appropriate military rank insignia in Bangladesh forces. "As we stood beside you in Desert Storm," they said in thanks, "now you stand beside us in our nation's time of need."[130] The following day, the JTF released PhibGru 3 and the 5th MEB.[131]

In less than two weeks ashore, the amphibious task force delivered 2,148 short tons of food, emergency medical supplies, water, clothing, and building materials. Marine aircraft flew 1,167 helicopter sorties in 1,114 flight hours to deliver 5,485 passengers and more than 695 tons of relief supplies. The average flight time per aircraft was 50.5 hours, about four times the normal operating tempo. The amphibious group's surface craft delivered 1,450 tons of relief aid.[132]

Much of what the amphibious task force accomplished ashore during Operation Sea Angel, however, was intangible. General Rowe felt that the Bangladesh relief effort was a visible demonstration of the effectiveness of democracy in action. Prime Minister Zia's government had been anxious to prove that a freely elected, responsible government could act swiftly and effectively in times of crisis. Sea Angel proved the ability of the Bangladesh government to take action, and showed how other world democracies were willing to provide immediate assistance in times of trouble. General Rowe also noted that the morning meetings and plenary sessions conducted by the command elements of the amphibious and joint task forces with civilian and military officials offered good role models and practical experience in democratic decision-making.[133]

In addition, both General Rowe and Admiral Clarey viewed Operation Sea Angel as a testament to the flexibility and capabilities of a forward-deployed amphibious force. Seldom in history have warriors been called upon to turn their swords into plowshares so quickly. Rapid planning, sea-based logistics, and over-the-horizon movement to shore were among the latest innovations in amphibious doctrine. Each of these capabilities was demonstrated in the Bay of Bengal.[134] The amphibious task force, General Stackpole remarked, was "the living embodiment of the true meaning of the 'Navy-Marine Corps Team.'

Coming from the sea you didn't intrude or overwhelm . . . . You supported and aided under the coordination of the Bangladesh fledgling democracy."[135] When combined with traditional Navy and Marine Corps devotion to duty and the individual skills of both Regular and Reserve Marines and sailors, the result was a hard-earned "well done" from Bangladesh and American officials alike. As Ambassador Milam noted: "There is no way to calculate how many scores of thousands of lives have been saved by your selfless labor. Be assured that the people of Bangladesh will never forget you, and nor will we Americans here, whom you have made so proud."[136]

Although the amphibious task force had been delayed on its return journey home, it appeared that not a single sailor or Marine resented this unexpected sojourn. Those who served on the shore were impressed by the tremendous resilience of the people of Bangladesh and the depth of the suffering they endured. None of these combat veterans remained unmoved by the forlorn look of starving and sick children, the plaintive cries of Bangladeshis who had lost family members, or the compassion of their comrades. General Rowe reported that all hands were visibly moved when poor Bangladeshis, most of whom had only two or three meager possessions, attempted to give one of them to the Americans as a gesture of gratitude.[137] Although the people of Bangladesh were unaware of it, the departing Marines had already been given the reward they wanted when they heard healthy children laughing or gazed at the smiles of thankful elders.[138] The sailors and Marines of the amphibious task force returned home with the self-satisfaction of knowing that when an unexpected call for help came, they were "good to go" and "made it happen."[139]

On 29 May, the amphibious cargo ship *St. Louis,* with the embarked Contingency Marine Air-Ground Task Force 2-91, commanded by Lieutenant Colonel Larry A. Johnson, rendezvoused with the departing amphibious task group. During the 10-day voyage, CMAGTF 2-91 Marines and corpsmen participated in a wide variety of training. They held classes on field hygiene, heat stress and first aid, and ROWPU operations, in addition to normal shipboard drills. Upon arrival they were provided with a detailed brief by members of the JTF Forward headquarters and the Bangladesh area military coordinator. The initial mooring off Cox's Bazar, however, proved fruitless, as the sailors and Marines sent ashore could not locate suitable LCM-8 landing sites due to an insufficient shore gradient and surf conditions. The *St. Louis* then steamed up the coast toward Chittagong.

During its two-week stay, the amphibious task group had operated more than 11 kilometers off the coast because of shallow water and numerous uncharted wrecks and shoals. Operating from such a great distance was impractical for the *St. Louis* and her LCM-8 landing craft. To function efficiently and safely, the amphibious cargo ship needed to be as close to the mouth of the Karnaphuli River as possible. To accomplish this, anchor buoys and drag lines were fabricated and a channel was swept through the line of 10 wrecks by two LCM-8 boats, clearing the way for the ship to anchor less than two kilometers from the port of Chittagong. This close-in anchorage, however, was not ideal. Fine, silt-

Department of Defense Photo (USN) DN-SC-85-06060

With the departure of the Amphibious Task Force, Contingency Marine Air-Ground Task Force 2-91, embarked on board the St. Louis *assumed the task of continuing the relief effort.*

laden water eventually permeated the ship's salt water systems, forcing the ship's engineers to work overtime, often in blistering heat, to keep the systems operational.[140]

Shortly after arriving off Chittagong, a CMAGTF 2-91 communications team and a small security element were sent ashore to support JTF operations. Offloading of the 28 reverse osmosis water purification units, Marine support teams, and their dispersal throughout the affected area began. As additional equipment and supplies were moved ashore to assist with the later retrograde of non-essential water purification units, floodlights, and generators, the ship's landing craft proceeded upriver to Chittagong where they delivered medical supplies, consisting of more than 600 cases of intravenous fluid, and 200 hot meals. Lieutenant Colonel Johnson, former operations officer of the 3d Force Service Support Group on Okinawa, also saw to it that members of CMAGTF 2-91 were rotated among the five water purification sites established by the task force's lead elements on Sandwip and Kutubdia Islands and at Chittagong.[141]

Despite a late start, "every Sailor and Marine aboard is happy to be here and they are ready for any tasking," reported Captain John W. Peterson, the *St. Louis*'s commanding officer.* However, replacing the eight-ship amphibious task group with one ship would be no easy task.[142] While some sailors performed routine duties on board the *St. Louis*, others shuttled medical supplies,

---

* Following the departure of the amphibious task group, Major General Stackpole designated Captain Peterson as the Naval Forces component commander and Lieutenant Colonel Johnson the Marine Forces component commander.

food, and equipment ashore and then returned with unneeded stores. The Marines and corpsmen of CMAGTF 2-91 were likewise tested. The Marines, in addition to delivering large amounts of food and medical supplies and producing and distributing thousands of gallons of potable water a day, provided satellite communications support, assuring the JTF a reliable form of communications when distance, topography, and weather affected all other means of communication. Officers and staff non-commissioned officers assisted with the basic support functions of the forward headquarters and U.S. Army and Air Force components, including the preparation of hot meals, routine health care, administrative support, insect control, and embarkation assistance. The attached corpsmen participated in a comprehensive assistance program, traveling to several impoverished villages and aiding those that were in need of medical attention. The contingency task force also established and operated arrival and departure airfield control groups at Zia International in Dhaka, which assured proper control of inbound supplies during the remaining days of the operation and coordination during the redeployment of JTF personnel and equipment.[143] With the arrival of the *St. Louis* and her "willing Sailors and the Marines of MAGTF 2-91, it gave us a balanced JTF as we ramp down and the Bangladeshi ramp up to take control of their destiny for the long haul."[144]

Relief operations proceeded smoothly as the month of May came to a close. The first phase of the campaign plan was completed in all but a few isolated

Photography courtesy of PhibGru 3

Operating the remaining water purification units was the primary job of contingency task force Marines. Each unit could produce more than 600 gallons of potable water an hour.

areas, while the second and third phases were well underway. The available aircraft, Air Force C-130s, Army Blackhawks, Japanese Dauphins, British Sea Kings, and recently integrated Bangladesh air force helicopters, were considered adequate to meet the demands. As outside donations slowly declined, the JTF's lift capability soon exceeded the amount of supplies on hand.

With the Government of Bangladesh beginning to assume an increasing share of the control and coordination of the relief effort, the gradual drawdown of personnel and equipment began. Among the first to be redeployed was the Joint Special Operations Task Force, followed by Army's 84th Engineer Detachment, elements of the Navy's Environmental and Preventative Medicine Unit, and a portion of Joint Task Force staff. The two Japanese Dauphin helicopters and an accompanying relief team departed on the 31st. In 76 missions, the two small Japanese helicopters had transported more than 21 tons of relief supplies. The *Fort Grange*, with its four Sea King helicopters and small boats, was scheduled to leave on 3 June.

Remaining elements of the Joint Task Force concentrated on providing assistance in three areas: the movement of food stocks from Dhaka to Chittagong; the distribution of relief supplies from central collection points and former LCAC ramps to outlying areas on Sandwip Island; and providing sustainment to the hardest-hit regions along the coast south of Chittagong. Although daily thunderstorms previously had caused slight delays, the relief effort had to be halted on the morning of 2 June. Located less than 200 nautical miles south southwest of Chittagong with winds of 110 kilometers per hour gusting to 130, Tropical Cyclone 03B was forecast to make landfall near or just north of the southern port city the following day. As a precaution, the *St. Louis* recovered ROWPU crews from all remote sites and then she and the *Fort Grange* moved out to sea.[*] The 374th Tactical Airlift Wing canceled all C-130 flights to Chittagong, stockpiles of food and water were secured, the Blackhawks were flown to Dhaka, the communications liaison team at Cox's Bazar was withdrawn, and the Chittagong Autovon/Autodin service was terminated. While underway, personnel on board the *St. Louis* took time to clean the ship and flush the engineering systems with clear water.[145]

The storm crossed the Patuakhali-Chittagong coast, northwest of the city, late on the 2d. Its measured wind speed of 100 kilometers per hour damaged crops and property along the coastal belt and off-shore islands. Low-lying areas again were inundated by a tidal surge measuring more than one meter. There were, however, no reported casualties.[146] "The Lord smiled on us today," noted General Stackpole, "as the anticipated new cyclone weakened on approach to

---

[*] While preparing to move to safer waters, the *Fort Grange* lost one of her four helicopters. All five crewmen were recovered safely, but several attempts by Bangladesh army and navy divers and the ship's mobile crane to salvage the aircraft were unsuccessful. (JTF-SA msg to USCinCPac, 021043ZJun91; *The New Nation*, Dhaka, 4Jun91).

landfall and had no significant impact on the already hard hit coastal and island area of southeast Bangladesh."[147]

On the morning of the 3d, the JTF reactivated relief operations, but at a slower pace. The *St. Louis* anchored off Chittagong at 0630, then returned key Marine personnel to the remote ROWPU sites to begin preparing the equipment for transport back to the ship. In addition to conducting boat operations, a 25-man joint Navy-Marine Corps working party moved ashore to help with the distribution of relief supplies and assisted the Air Force's 4th Combat Communications Group to strike its base camp at Chittagong. As C-130 flight operations between Dhaka and Chittagong resumed, four of the five UH-60 Blackhawks returned to Chittagong and began the process of backloading ROWPUs, redistributing rice on Sandwip Island, and delivering medical supplies as needed. However, helicopter flight operations were limited to four hours per aircraft per day in order to keep all four aircraft functioning. Shortly before noon, the *Fort Grange* and her contingent of Royal Marines departed the waters off Chittagong enroute to Colombo. In 10 days, the British sailors and Marines had "shifted a total of 99 metric tonnes of food, medical and building supplies."[148]

With conditions in the affected area gradually returning to normal and the Government of Bangladesh assuming an ever-greater role in the relief effort, the JTF continued to draw down. General Stackpole's redeployment plan called for the withdrawal of personnel and equipment from all outlying areas to Dhaka or the *St. Louis*, the departure of non-essential personnel and equipment by daily Military Airlift Command C-141 sustainment flights, and the termination of operations at Chittagong by 7 June. Between the 7th and the 13th all remaining JTF personnel and equipment would be withdrawn.[149]

By 4 June, the remaining ROWPUs and their supporting equipment and personnel, except for one which supplied water to the forward headquarters at Chittagong, were extracted from Sandwip and Kutubdia Islands and transported by helicopter and then landing craft to the *St. Louis*. During more than three weeks of operation, the water purification units had produced and distributed more than 266,000 gallons of potable water. The retrograde of personnel and equipment, interspersed with a number of relief missions, continued the following day, despite strong isolated showers and thunderstorms.

On the 6th, all air relief operations came to an end when Army helicopters flew from Chittagong to Dhaka, and the 374th Tactical Airlift Wing completed its last C-130 mission, delivering more than 74 tons of rice for the Red Crescent Society to Chittagong. Both C-130s, along with the first increment of the 4th Combat Communications Group, departed on 8 June. They were followed two days later by the 25th Infantry Division's five UH-60 Blackhawk helicopters.[150] During three weeks of flying, the Army Blackhawks logged 805 sorties and carried more than 885 tons of relief supplies. Air Force HC-130 and C-130 aircraft flew 194 sorties, and transported 2,430 tons of supplies to Chittagong and the flood-ravaged Sylhet region of northeastern Bangladesh.[151]

On 7 June, with the withdrawal of personnel and equipment to Dhaka complete, the forward headquarters at Chittagong was closed. Later in the day, the JTF released the *St. Louis* and CMAGTF 2-91 from their duties as Naval and Marine Force components.[152] However, because of monsoon rains, reduced visibility, and heavy traffic, the *St. Louis* was unable to get underway on the evening tide.

In his final report to General Stackpole the following morning, Lieutenant Colonel Johnson noted that "during the past two days I have had ample opportunity to reflect back on the past three weeks and to have considered our contributions. Without a doubt, each and every member of CMAGTF 2-91 is most pleased that he had an opportunity to participate in the relief operation and to have helped the citizens of Bangladesh. However," he continued, "we wish we could have provided even more support. I suppose this is natural given the average American's penchant for generosity. As we depart the AOR, and speaking for all of my Marines and Corpsmen, we leave behind new-found friends, many memories, and, most importantly, our prayers for the Bangladesh people. It was an honor to serve."[153]

Early on the 8th, the *St. Louis* weighed anchor and steamed for Phuket, Thailand, where her crew was granted its first liberty in weeks. Four days later as the ship left Phuket, her tasking again was changed. On orders from Seventh Fleet, the *St. Louis* was to make the best possible speed to Subic Bay in the Philippines. There she and her embarked Marines would provide humanitarian assistance to the naval base and nearby Cubi Point Naval Air Station after the volcanic eruption of Mount Pinatubo, followed by several days of torrential rains and severe earthquakes.[154]

With the departure of the *St. Louis*, General Stackpole declared the second phase of the campaign plan complete. It was, he reported to Pacific Command, a "superb effort by all involved [which] produced unprecedented relief. Safety was paramount; mission accomplished without any injury to U.S. personnel or loss of equipment."[155] During the next five days, the remaining 190 members of the JTF and their equipment were flown by Air Force C-141s and C-5As to their home stations on Hawaii, Okinawa, and Guam. Following a news conference at which Ambassador Milam and General Stackpole presided, the commander of the JTF boarded the last C-5A for the flight home to Okinawa. On 14 June, Pacific Command terminated Operation Sea Angel and formally deactivated the Joint Task Force.[156]

"Words really can't convey the depth of our feeling here," noted Ambassador William Milam in his message to Admiral Charles Larson, "our gratitude and fond wishes to Major General Henry C. Stackpole, III, and all the officers and enlisted personnel comprising JTF Operation Sea Angel. All deserve the highest, strongest commendation for their superlative relief operation in Bangladesh." The Joint Task Force, he continued, "admirably fulfilled its mission of bringing food to the starving, medicine to the sick, and hope to the hopeless. But coincident to its mission, JTFSA also served the foreign interests of the United States by very visibly enabling a fledgling democracy to meet the most critical

Photograph courtesy of American Embassy, Dhaka

MajGen Stackpole and American Ambassador Milam brief reporters at the Dhaka embassy on the accomplishments of the relief effort.

needs of a distressed population." While General Stackpole had become a legend in Bangladesh for his "leadership, sensitivity, and high intelligence," it was "the superior organization and efficiency of JTFSA, the unusual professional competence of its members, as well as their unfailingly sympathetic and benign behavior on foreign soil [that] brought great credit to their services, to themselves, to this mission, and to our country."[157]   General Colin Powell echoed Ambassador Milam's words: "The magnificent performance of every Sailor, Marine, Soldier, Airman left an indelible mark on nearly two million people who will never forget 'The Angels From the Sea.'   The end results of

'Sea Angel' are lives saved, the enhanced faith of a people in its democratic government, and 'a view of America as truly a friend in time of need.'"[158]

Praise also came from Bangladeshi officials, both civilian and military. Among the many tributes, the one written by Muhammad Omar Farooq, zonal relief coordinator for Cox's Bazar, expressed the sentiments of all:

> Today, democracy in our country is reborn. It is young, hardly a few months old. But within these few months it has had its baptism of fire, with the fateful and devastating Cyclone and Tidal surge of 29 April 1991, which rocked our people to their roots and caused devastation on a scale hitherto unknown, and left them in a state of complete shock and bewilderment.
>
> But our people are resilient, they are born in cyclones and tidal bores, and they grow and live with them. For them, cyclones and tidal bores are almost so to say a natural habitat. With fortitude, and indomitable courage our people withstood the scourge of the cyclone which was like a holocaust. Inspiration and unshakable assistance from friends like you helped to get us back on our feet sooner than later, and move boldly ahead. You and your sea angels, helped, facilitated and expedited the process of our recovery. For this, we will remain indebted. We have no words adequate to express our gratitude.[159]

Photograph courtesy of RAdm Stephen S. Clarey, USN (Ret)

The smiling faces of young Bangladeshi villagers near Cox's Bazar was, as RAdm Stephen S. Clarey later said, a testament to the efforts of American Marines, seamen, airmen, and soldiers.

Operation Sea Angel, Stackpole later noted, "was a significant chapter in U.S. history because . . . it was the forerunner of what caused us to go to Somalia." If the Bangladesh relief operation had been a failure, "you would not see anywhere near the interested effort going on for these other rescue operations. But it became," he continued, "a model in the sense of how we construct the task force; a model in the sense of not having an . . . intrusive element with a large footprint because we come from the sea; a model in respect for sovereignty; and a model in campaign planning." A goal was set and "we achieved the goal," he concluded, "and we created the conditions in each phase necessary to move to the next phase."[160]

Epilogue

At its peak, more than 7,500 American military personnel were involved in the relief effort. In slightly more than four weeks of operations almost 2,000 helicopter and C-130 sorties were flown, carrying 4,000 tons of supplies--more than 1,500 tons were delivered by surface craft. More than 1.7 million people were reached and aided in the affected area and thousands of lives were saved from the ravages of disease and starvation. "When we left Bangladesh," General Stackpole later noted, "the crops were growing and the trees had sprouted leaves, . . . and there was life in the area."[161]

Joint Task Force Sea Angel's legacy was more than healed bodies and full stomachs, it also left behind a reservoir of knowledge and recommendations. Elements of the task force produced harbor assessment and embankment engineering studies and updated local physicians in disease treatment and patient care. "The salutary effect of the Task Force effort," Stackpole reported, "has been a study by the Government of Bangladesh of our organization, structure, equipment and methodologies for adoption where possible for their own civil/military disaster plan." However, more needed to be done. In his last situation report to Pacific Command, Major General Stackpole noted that while much remained to be done in Bangladesh, he believed that the United States had a future training opportunity. He recommended that disaster relief ties be maintained with Bangladesh and that "technical help from [the United States] military in form of MTT's [mobile training teams] and medical expertise appears to be the way to go."[162]

Disaster relief ties were maintained and would be tested in November 1992 as Tropical Cyclone Forest moved up the Bay of Bengal toward the offshore islands and coastal lowlands of southeastern Bangladesh, the same area devastated more than a year earlier. While the Bangladesh government alerted its citizenry and mobilized its armed forces, the American government also took action. Pacific Command was alerted that it, when directed by the President, would provide "support for relief operations to assist the Government of Bangladesh in recovering from tropical cyclone damage for a period of approximately 2 weeks."[163]

Early on the morning of 20 November, CinCPac activated a crisis planning group and subsequently designated Major General Donald R. Gardner, General Stackpole's successor at III Marine Expeditionary Force, to be Commander, Joint Task Force Bangladesh Relief.[164] During the next 24 hours, III MEF activated a crisis action center and provided the Pacific Command estimates of the situation and of forces that would be needed.[165] As planning moved ahead and operation orders were written, Joint Task Force Bangladesh Relief was redesignated Joint Task Force Sea Angel II and Navy, Marine, Army, and Air Force units were assigned and alerted.[166] Despite the extensive planning and preparations, Joint Task Force Sea Angel II did not deploy because Tropical Cyclone Forest made landfall approximately 230 kilometers southeast of Chittagong in Burma. The damage in Bangladesh was much less than had been anticipated, so Ambassador William Milam did not expect any request for disaster relief because the Bangladesh government was better prepared this time around.[167] The seeds of Sea Angel bore fruit within the first year.

The disaster relief ties between Bangladesh and the United States did not end with Sea Angel II. In May 1992, CinCPac inaugurated the Joint/Combined Exchange Training Program and designated the Pacific Special Operations Command to be the executive agency for planning, coordinating, and conducting exercises and training for active and Reserve Army, Navy, Marine, Air Force, and Special Operations personnel throughout the Pacific. Two months after Tropical Cyclone Forest struck, American soldiers, sailors, and airmen were deployed to Bangladesh to share and improve upon combined American and Bangladesh disaster relief techniques. The Bangladesh Defense Forces handled most of the nation's disaster relief efforts, so the American teams were to train with Bangladeshi forces and provide instruction in aerial delivery, pathfinder operations, piloting techniques, underwater search and salvage, hydrographic survey, and underwater demolitions.[168]

The "Balance Buffalo" series of exercises, two of which were conducted in 1993, continued. The training deployment of one Special Forces detachment from the 1st Battalion, 1st Special Forces Group (Airborne), one C-130 from the 374th Air Wing, and a four-man civil affairs direct support team from the 426th Civil Affairs Battalion in April 1994 proved fortuitous. Shortly after they arrived in Bangladesh, a major cyclone began moving toward the coast. The American Embassy indicated that if the devastation was similar to that of the April 1991 storm, they might again ask CinCPac for assistance. Without hesitation the American forces moved into action, dispatching the C-130 from the training site to Dhaka where a special forces team prepared to provide a secure communications link to the embassy, if required, for the coordination of the disaster relief effort. However, like Cyclone Forest, the 1994 storm veered south and crossed the coast near the border with Burma. The 374th Air Wing's C-130 provided overflight and reconnaissance to the ambassador and country team, assisting with the damage assessment. The devastation was relatively light, consisting primarily of property damage, and the embassy determined that no additional support would be required.[169]

With ongoing training exercises like Balance Buffalo, the response of Bangladesh civilian agencies and armed forces will improve and combined relief efforts, in the event of a future disaster, will be easier. In addition, the USAID mission resident in Dhaka along with United Nations and other bilateral agencies have a continuous program with Bangladesh civilian agencies to strengthen both disaster preparedness and relief programs. Although Bangladesh, with its unique geography and climate, will continue to be battered by natural disasters, future disaster relief operations should result in less loss of life, livestock, and property than in the past as a result of the lessons learned during Operation Sea Angel.

Notes

Unless otherwise noted, the material in this monograph was derived from: 5th MEB After Action Report "The 5th MEB Deployment to SWA, 2 August 1990-29 May 1991," hereafter 5th MEB AAR; 5th MEB Staff interview by LtCol Ronald J. Brown conducted at 5th MEB HQ, Camp Pendleton, California, 25Jul91, hereafter 5th MEB intvw; 5th MEB Operations Brief, hereafter 5th MEB Ops Brief; MAG-50 ComdC, Mar-Jun91; MAG-50 Special Action Report, "Sea Angel: Case Study," hereafter MAG-50 SAR; LtGen Henry C. Stackpole III, "Angels from the Sea," *U.S. Naval Institute Proceedings*, May92, pp. 110-16, hereafter Stackpole, "Angels from the Sea"; BGen Peter J. Rowe, "Interview," *U.S. Naval Institute Proceedings*, May92, pp. 128-132; LtCol Donald R. Selvage, "Operation Sea Angel: Bangladesh Disaster Relief," *Marine Corps Gazette*, Nov91, pp. 89-97; and "Bangladesh--Cyclone," *OFDA Annual Report FY 1991*, pp. 18-24. Source materials used in the preparation of this volume are located in the "Sea Angel Files," Archives Section, Marine Corps Historical Center, Washington, D.C.

1. Vernon Loeb, "Again, calamity, familiar guest in an unlucky land," *Philadelphia Inquirer*, 5May91, hereafter Loeb, "Again, calamity."

2. Capt Shafiq-ur-Rahman, Bangladesh Navy, "Disaster in Bangladesh: A Multinational Relief Effort," *Naval War College Review*, Winter93, pp. 59-62.

3. Caritas Bangladesh, *Cyclone 1991*, 5May91, p. 3, in MajGen Henry C. Stackpole III, Final Report of Operation Sea Angel, 20Jun91, hereafter Stackpole, "Final Report," 20Jun91.

4. 5th MEB, "Angels From the Sea: A Case Study of 5th Marine Expeditionary Brigade's Humanitarian Assistance to Bangladesh, May 1991," undated, p. 1, hereafter 5th MEB, "Case Study."

5. Caritas Bangladesh, *Cyclone 1991: An Appeal*, 11May91, p. 5, in Stackpole, "Final Report," 20Jun91.

6. AmEmbassy, Dhaka msg to SecState, 301216ZApr91.

7. AmEmbassy, Dhaka msg to SecState, 010737ZMay91; SecState msg to AmEmbassy, Dhaka, 030503ZMay91.

8. Brig Ibrahim Ahmed and Col A. Md. Moazzem, "Disaster Preparedness In Bangladesh and Role of Bangladesh Army in Disaster Management," (Paper given at Military Operations and Law Conference, Honolulu, Hawaii, 16-19Sept91), pp. 18-19.

9. AmEmbassy, Dhaka msg to SecState, 030752ZMay91; AmEmbassy, Dhaka msg to SecState, 030948ZMay91.

10. USDAO, Dhaka msg to JCS/SecDef, 020736ZMay91.

11. AmEmbassy, Dhaka msg to SecState, 030948ZMay91.

12. Ibid.

13. USDAO, Dhaka msg to JCS/SecDef, 020736ZMay91.

14. Loeb, "Again, calamity."

15. U.S. President, *Public Papers of the Presidents of the United States* (Washington: Office of the *Federal Register*, National Archives, 1992), George Bush, 1991, v. 1, p. 463.

16. AmEmbassy, Dhaka msg to SecState, 041212ZMay91.

17. Ibid.

18. Caritas Bangladesh, *Cyclone 1991*, 5May91, p. 6, in Stackpole, "Final Report," 20Jun91.

19. AmEmbassy, Dhaka msg to SecState, 041212ZMay91.

20. SecState msg to AmEmbassy, Dhaka 040420ZMay91.

21. AmEmbassy, Dhaka msg to SecState, 041212ZMay91; AmEmbassy, Dhaka msg to SecState, 061123ZMay91.

22. USDAO, Dhaka msg to DIA, 220852ZJul91.

23. AmEmbassy, Dhaka msg to SecState, 061201ZMay91.

24. Ibid.; AmEmbassy, Dhaka msg to SecState, 051208ZMay91.

25. USDAO, Dhaka msg to USCinCPac, 060445ZMay91.

26. USDAO, Dhaka msg to USCinCPac, 060507ZMay91.

27. USDAO, Dhaka msg to DIA, 220852ZMay91.

28. 5th MEB, ComdC, 18Mar-30Jun91.

29. SecState msg to AmEmbassy, Dhaka, 080357ZMay91.

30. AmEmbassy, Dhaka msg to SecState, 081238ZMay91.

31. 5th MEB, AAR.

32. ComSeventhFlt msg to ComPhibGru 3, 5th MEB, and CTF 76, 080513ZMay91.

33. ComPhibGru 3 msg to ComSeventhFlt, 082001ZMay91.

34. CTF 76 msg to ComSeventhFlt, 081600ZMay91.

35. USCinCPac msg to USDAO, Dhaka, 090015ZMay91.

36. USDAO, Dhaka msg to USCinCPac, 060657ZMay91.

37. CJTF Sea Angel, "Final Report on Operation Sea Angel, 20Jun91; USDAO, Dhaka msg to USCinCPac, 080731ZMay91; USDAO, Dhaka msg to DIA, 22Jul91.

38. AmEmbassy, Dhaka msg to SecState, 091113ZMay91.

39. USDAO, Dhaka msg to USCinCPac, 091117ZMay91.

40. USCinCPac msg to AmEmbassy, Dhaka, 092345ZMay91.

41. LtCol Gary W. Anderson, USMC, "Operation Sea Angel; A Retrospective on the 1991 Humanitarian Relief Operation in Bangladesh," (Naval War College), Rpt 1-92, 15Jan92, pp. 5-6, hereafter Anderson, "Sea Angel."

42. Col Stephen E. Lindblom, Comments on draft ms, 20Apr95, hereafter Lindblom Comments.

43. AmEmbassy, Dhaka msg to SecState, 111220ZMay91.

44. USDAO, Dhaka msg to USCinCPac, 101340ZMay91.

45. *New York Times*, 12May91, p. 6.

46. Joint Staff memo to CJCS, 10May91.

47. DepSec memo to CJCS, 10May91.

48. Joint Staff msg to USCinCPac, 102323ZMay91.

49. USCinCPac msg to AmEmbassy, Dhaka, 110315ZMay91.

50. Stackpole, "Final Report," 20Jun91.

51. USCinCPac msg to AmEmbassy, Dhaka, 110315ZMay91; USCinCPac msg to Joint Staff, 110325ZMay91.

52. USCinCPac msg to USCinCPacFlt, 110315ZMay91.

53. *New York Times*, 12May91, pp. 1, 6.

54. CJCS msg to USCinCPac, 111315ZMay91.

55. Stackpole, "Angels from the Sea," p. 112; LtGen Henry C. Stackpole III, "Operation Sea Angel: Marine Corps Relief Operations in Bangladesh," MCHC Seminar, 30Jan92, hereafter Stackpole, "MCHC Sea Angel Seminar," 30Jan92.

56. JTF-PE msg to USDAO, Dhaka, 110724ZMay91.

57. USDAO, Dhaka msg to JTF-PE, 111211ZMay91.

58. Anderson, "Sea Angel," pp. 6-8; USCinCPac msg to CinCPacFlt, 111734ZMay91; ComSeventhFlt msg to CTG 76.6, 110930ZMay91.

59. Anderson, "Sea Angel," p. 8.

60. JTF-PE msg to USDAO, Dhaka, 110724ZMay91.

61. Anderson, "Sea Angel," p. 9; Stackpole, "MCHC Sea Angel Seminar," 30Jan92.

62. USDAO msg to JTF-PE, 111211ZMay91; JTF-PE msg to USCinCPac, 121739ZMay91.

63. Ibid.

64. USCinCPac msg to CdrUSAPac, 111204ZMay91; 353 SOW msg to COMSocPac, 121247ZMay91; JTF-PE msg to USCinCPac, 130814ZMay91; Anderson, "Sea Angel," pp. 11-12; Cdr 1/1SFGA msg to Cdr 4thSOSC, 110650ZJun91.

65. JTF-PE msg to USCinCPac, 130814ZMay91.

66. Stackpole, "MCHC Sea Angel Seminar," 30Jan92.

67. Stackpole, "Final Report," 20Jun91.

68. JTF-PE msg to USCinCPac, 130814ZMay91.

69. JTF-PE msg to USCinCPac, 130814ZMay91.

70. Ibid.

71. JTF-PE msg to USCinCPac, 141629ZMay91.

72. Stackpole, "MCHC Sea Angel Seminar," 30Jan92.

73. JTF-PE msg to USCinCPac, 141629ZMay91.

74. AmEmbassy, Dhaka msg to SecState, 131245ZMay91.

75. 374 AW Hist, Jan-Jun91, p. 44.

76. MOA, JTFSA and American Embassy, Dhaka, undated.

77. Amb William B. Milam, Comments on draft ms, 18Feb95.

78. JTF-PE msg to USCinCPac, 141629ZMay91; USDAO, Dhaka msg to DIA, 220852ZJul91; and LtCol Anderson, "Sea Angel," pp. 13-14.

79. JTF-PE msg to USCinCPac, 141629ZMay91.

80. JTF-PE msg to USCinCPac, 141640ZMay91.

81. USCinCPac msg to USCinCPacFlt, 130904ZMay91; USCinCPac msg to USCinCPacFlt, 140534ZMay91; USS *St Louis* (LKA 116) 1991 Command History, 23Mar91.

82. CG III MEF msg to CG 3d MarDiv, 160021ZMay91.

83. CMAGTF 2-91, ComdC 16May-8Jul91, dtd 3Jul91.

84. Stackpole, "MCHC Sea Angel Seminar," 30Jan92.

85. BGen Peter J. Rowe, Comments on draft ms, 23Feb95, hereafter Rowe Comments; Col Stephen E. Lindblom, Comments on draft ms, 20Apr95.

86. JTF-PE msg to USCinCPac, 152326ZMay91.

87. Stackpole, "Final Report," 20Jun91.

88. Ibid.

89. USCinCPac msg to USCinCPacFlt, 161152ZMay91.

90. 5th MEB Ops Brief.

91. Ibid.

92. Col Drake F. Trumpe, 5th MEB intvw.

93. 5th MEB intvw.

94. 5th MEB AAR.

95. MAG-50 SAR.

96. USS *Tarawa*, 1991 Command History, 3Apr92.

97. 5th MEB intvw.

98. Rowe Comments.

99. Stackpole, "MCHC Sea Angel Seminar," 30Jan92.

100. USS *Tarawa*, 1991 Command History, 3Apr92.

101. 5th MEB Ops Brief.

102. 5th MEB, "Case Study"; 5th MEB intvw.

103. Rowe Comments.

104. Rowe Comments.

105. 374 AW Hist, Jan-Jun91, p. 44.

106. Stackpole, "Final Report," 20Jun91.

107. MAG-50 SAR.

108. Ibid.

109. LtCol Kevin M. Kennedy ltr to authors, 4Aug93.

110. Stackpole, "MCHC Sea Angel Seminar," 30Jan92.

111. JO3 J. Vincent Dickens, USN, "Relief Helicopters Fill Up at 'Bob's,'" *Leatherneck*, Sep91, p. 17.

112. USCinCPac msg to AmEmbassy, Dhaka, 130804ZMay91.

113. CG, 5th MEB msg to ComSeventhFlt, 301535ZMay91; 2dLt J. W. Disney, "Sea Angels Dropped Food and Supplies," *Leatherneck*, Sep91, pp. 15-16.

114. BGen Randall L. West, Comments on draft ms, 10Apr95, hereafter West Comments.

115. JTF-SA msg to JTF-SA (FWD), 220353ZMay91.

116. Stackpole, "MCHC Sea Angel Seminar," 30Jan92.

117. 539 AS, Operation Manna, Post Operation Report, 10Jun91.

118. "Memorandum of Understanding Between the Government of the People's Republic of Bangladesh and the United States of America to Specify the Legal Status of the United States Pacific Command Disaster Relief Task Force," 20May91.

119. Joint Staff msg to USCinCPac, 17May91.

120. Stackpole, "MCHC Sea Angel Seminar," 30Jan92.

121. NEPMU 6, 1991 Command History, 26Feb92.

122. Dr. John R. Downs, "Historical Medical Perspective: Operation Sea Angel, Bangladesh Relief Effort," undated.

123. 2/11, ComdC, 18Mar-30Jun91.

124. 5th MEB, "Case Study."

125. Ibid.

126. Stackpole, "Final Report," 20Jun91.

127. U. S. President, *Public Papers of the Presidents of the United States* (Washington: Office of the *Federal Register*, National Archives, 1992), George Bush, 1991, v. 1, p. 574.

128. SecState msg to AmEmbassy, 1302217ZJun91; USCinCPac msg to SecDef, 180255ZJun91.

129. JTF-SA msg to USCinCPac, 281613ZMay91.

130. West Comments.

131. CG, 5thMEB msg to ComSeventhFlt, 301535ZMay91.

132. MAG-50, ComdC, 18Mar-30Jun91; Phibron 3, Command History, 1991, dtd Mar92.

133. 5th MEB intvw.

134. 5th MEB, ComdC, 18Mar-30Jun91.

135. JTF-SA msg to ComPhibGru 3, 281422ZMay91.

136. CG, 5thMEB msg to ComSeventhFlt, 301535ZMay91.

137. Rowe intvw, p. 131.

138. 2dLt James W. Disney, "MAG-50 Marines Finish the Rescue Missions," *Okinawa Marine*, 21Jun91, p. 8.

139. 5th MEB, ComdC, 18Mar-30Jun91.

140. USS *St Louis*, 1991 Command History, 23Mar91.

141. CTG 76.4 msg to JTF-SA, 301710ZMay91; CMAGTF 2-91 msg to JTF-SA, 010930Jun91.

142. CTG 76.4 msg to JTF-SA, 301710ZMay91.

143. CMAGTF 2-91, ComdC, 3Jul91.

144. JTF-SA msg to USCinCPac, 032330ZJun91.

145. USS *St Louis* msg to JTF-SA, 021710ZJun91.

146. USCinCPac msg to Joint Staff, 030154ZJun91.

147. JTF-SA msg to USCinCPac, 022215ZJun91.

148. Sgt P. J. Webb, "Operation Manna," *The Globe & Laurel: The Journal of the Royal Marines*, Jul/Aug91, p. 237.

149. USCinCPac msg to Joint Staff, 040134ZJun91.

150. JTF-SA msg to USCinCPac, 080843ZJun91.

151. JTF-SA msg to USCinCPac, 090903ZJun91.

152. JTF-SA msg to USS *St Louis*, 070800ZJun91.

153. CMAGTF 2-91 msg to JTF-SA, 081525ZJun91.

154. USS *St Louis*, 1991 Command History, 23Mar92; CMAGTF 2-91, ComdC, 3Jul91.

155. JTF-SA msg to USCinCPac, 080450ZJun91.

156. USCinCPac msg to CinCPacFlt, 140734ZJun91.

157. AmEmbassy, Dhaka msg to USCinCPac, 161158ZJun91.

158. CJCS msg to USCinCPac, 131005ZJun91.

159. Muhammad Omar Farooq ltr to MajGen Stackpole, 6Jun91.

160. LtGen Henry C. Stackpole, intvw, 29Apr93.

161. Stackpole, "MCHC Sea Angel Seminar," 30Jan92.

162. JTF-SA msg to USCinCPac, 131157ZMay91.

163. CJCS msg to USCinCPac, 192345ZNov92.

164. USCinCPac msg to CG, III MEF, 200430ZNov92.

165. CG, III MEF msg to USCinCPac, 200320ZNov92; CG, III MEF msg to USCinCPac, 201110ZNov92.

166. USCinCPac msg to COMMarForPac, 210610ZNov92.

167. USCinCPac msg to Joint Staff, 211730ZNov92.

168. ComSocPac msg to USCinCPac, 080113ZApr93; ComSocPac msg to USCinCPac, 080201ZJul93; Sgt Weston Ochse, USA, and Sgt Andrew Gudgel, USA, "Disaster Relief Crosstraining: Bangladesh 1993," *Asia-Pacific Defense Forum*, Sum93, pp. 37-41.

169. ComSocPac, "Background--Balance Buffalo 94-2," 4May94.

Appendix A
Chronology

29-30 April 1991--Tropical Cyclone 02B, Marian, devastates coastal region of Bangladesh. The port of Chittagong and the city of Cox's Bazar severely damaged and the islands of South Hatia, Sandwip, Kutubdia, and Manpura submerged. Water and power distribution systems, tubewells, housing, and transportation infrastructure badly damaged.

30 April--Bangladeshi Prime Minister Begum Khaleda Zia, after visiting the affected area, appeals to international community "to come forward in aid of humanity in distress." Thirty-two countries respond with some form of assistance.

U.S. Ambassador William B. Milam declares disaster in Bangladesh and provides $25,000 for disaster relief and releases 5,500 pounds of Department of Defense (DOD) donated medical supplies.

1 May--Ambassador Milam visits affected area with other chiefs of mission.

2 May--Bangladeshi armed forces and military medical units deployed to affected districts.

U.S. Agency for International Development donates 727,000 water purification tablets to Bangladesh government and non-government agencies for distribution.

3 May--President George Bush informs Prime Minister Zia that the United States stands ready to assist. USAID Director and U.S. Defense Attache and military staff visit affected areas.

5 May--Bangladeshi naval vessels reach Sandwip, Manpura, and Kutubdia Islands after earlier attempts were thwarted by heavy seas.

6 May--Additional Bangladeshi military assets deployed to area.

Ambassador Milam queries Commander in Chief, Pacific (CinCPac) about the possible use of Navy and Marine Corps air and surface assets to assist in the relief effort.

8 May--Deployment of 15 U.S. Corps of Engineer personnel already in-country to Chittagong to assist in rehabilitation of airport.

9 May--III Marine Expeditionary Force (MEF) receives indications from Fleet Marine Force, Pacific (FMFPac) that the MEF was one candidate being considered as the nucleus for a proposed joint task force to assist in relief efforts. CG, III MEF, MajGen Henry C. Stackpole III, in Philippines attending Seventh Fleet planning conference. III MEF planning cell formed to follow situation and develop a series of options.

10 May--Air Force C-141 from Okinawa and C-5A from Southwest Asia arrive at Dhaka with DOD-donated relief supplies.

11 May--President George Bush announces decision to go beyond the financial support rendered by the U.S. Embassy and to dispatch a joint task force to Bangladesh. Commander in Chief, Pacific, Admiral Charles R. Larson, would exercise overall responsibility for the operation, codenamed Productive Effort, while MajGen Stackpole was designated Joint Task Force (JTF) commander. The relief effort was to be phased:

Phase I: Form and deploy JTF to assess situation and recommend concept of operations.

Phase II: Deploy command, control, and communications equipment and personnel, civil affairs and disaster assessment teams, medical personnel, and helicopters to facilitate assessment and provide immediate assistance.

Phase III: Employ Amphibious Group 3 (PhibGru 3) and embarked 5th Marine Expeditionary Brigade (MEB) to provide additional helicopters, water transport, communications, and support personnel and equipment.

PhibGru 3, enroute from Persian Gulf to West Coast, diverted to support relief operations.

2100, the 28-man Survey and Reconnaissance (Advance) Party, headed by MajGen Stackpole, departs Kadena AFB, Okinawa, on board a C-141 for Dhaka.

12 May--0700, JTF Advance Party arrives in Dhaka, is briefed by Ambassador Milam and staff, and sets up housekeeping in a rented house on the outskirts of the capital. Satellite communications established with CinCPac in Hawaii and III MEF on Okinawa.

Initial assessment was that distribution was the primary problem facing the relief effort. Food and supplies would have to be moved to Chittagong and then to outlying areas; water, food, and medical needs could be met within two weeks, but an additional two weeks would be needed to stabilize overall health crisis.

Elements of 1st Battalion, First Special Forces Group (Airborne), arrives from Okinawa on board two C-130s. The aircraft are committed to airlifting bulk supplies from Dhaka to Chittagong.

13 May--MajGen Stackpole and staff visit disaster area on board two Bangladeshi air force UH-1 helicopters, accompanied by several host country military officers, Ambassador Milam, the USAID Director, and the embassy pubic affairs officer. Assessment was that food supplies were adequate and that a combination of helicopters, landing craft, and air drops should be effective in distributing the food. Focus was on identifying and moving personnel and equipment into the area as quickly as possible.

JTF augmentation cell arrives from Hawaii. Cell included designated deputy, Col Edward G. Hoffman, USAF, who was also designated the Air Force Component Commander. Also included were five U.S. Army UH-60 Blackhawk helicopters, along with Seabee assets and an environmental medicine unit.

Commander, Joint Task Force (CJTF) decides to split staff between Dhaka and Chittagong. Col Stephen E. Lindbolm, III MEF G-3, would remain in Dhaka as JTF Chief of Staff. Col Mike Ferguson, USAF, designated Chief of Staff at JTF (Forward) in Chittagong. Headquarters at Dhaka moved to unused Bangladeshi air force barracks at old airfield outside capital; initial building retained as press headquarters.

St. Louis ordered to Okinawa to load 28 ROWPUs (water purification units) and support personnel and to proceed to Bangladesh.

14 May--CJTF visits disaster sites with Ambassador, USAID Director, embassy PAO, and senior members of Bangladesh command staff.

15 May--JTF establishes forward headquarters and air detachment at Chittagong to coordinate relief efforts in the hardest hit areas.

First formal meeting of the Combined Relief Tasking Cell. Representatives from the JTF, U.S. Embassy, AID, CARE, Red Crescent, and Bangladeshi military, civil, and non-governmental assistance agencies attend. Daily meeting of Cell continued until 28 May when it was determined that adequate supplies had been delivered to Chittagong and that further meetings would be conducted as needed.

Disaster relief and communications teams and first relief supplies delivered to remote disaster sites.

PhibGru 3, composed of eight ships, commanded by RAdm Stephen S. Clarey, and 5th MEB under the command of BGen Peter J. Rowe, arrives off coast of Bangladesh.

16 May--PhibGru 3 and 5th MEB, augmented by a Japanese contingent, began full-scale relief efforts. Twenty-eight helicopters, in conjunction with four LCACs and three LCUs, handled the bulk of local distribution of food and medical supplies in the area of Chittagong, Sandwip, Kutubdia, and Moheshkheli.

17 May--Campaign plan approved and implemented:

Phase I: Immediate efforts to stabilize life-threatening situations (14 days).

Phase II: Delivery of supplies and equipment that would allow government and people to assume control of relief efforts (10 days).

Phase III: Preparation for U.S. withdrawal and the assumption of full control of relief efforts by the Government of Bangladesh (5 days).

18 May--Eight of a total of 36 ROWPUs arrive and are located at Chittagong. Two units became operational on Kutubdia Island on 20 May, while two units are shipped to Sandwip Island and are placed in service on the 24th.

19 May--First of six 5th MEB MedCap teams deployed.

   Second control center established at Cox's Bazar by Marine Battalion Landing Team 3/5.

20 May--RFA *Fort Grange* arrives off Cox's Bazar with elements of 539 Assault Squadron, Royal Marines, on board.

21 May--Operations under campaign plan proceeding; phase one essentially complete despite daily thunderstorms and occasional tornadoes.

   Mrs. Marilyn Quayle, wife of U.S. Vice President, arrives for three-day visit. During visit operational codename redesignated Sea Angel.

29 May--Phase II nears completion, transition back to a primarily Bangladeshi effort underway, and PhibGru 3 and 5th MEB depart.

   St. Louis, with 28 ROWPUs embarked, arrives to act as interim platform during completion of Phase II. Marine Air-Ground Task Force 2-91, commanded by LtCol Larry A. Johnson, configured as a humanitarian relief unit on board to act as a partial replacement for the amphibious task force.

30 May--In-country force drawdown begins; all personnel to be out of country by 13 June.

2 June--Tropical Cyclone 03B comes ashore northwest of Chittagong, but causes no loss of life or serious damage.

4 June--All forces returned to forward locations and continue operations.

7 June--Emphasis changes to retrograde. Helicopter relief operations completed. All available government and non-government supplies delivered. Situation returning to normal with road networks, ferry boats, and local infrastructure being returned to pre-cyclone conditions.

   St. Louis departs for Thailand. Last day of operations at Chittagong.

13 June--Redeployment of all personnel and equipment completed.

15 June--Operation Sea Angel terminated.

Appendix B
Command and Staff List

Joint Task Force Sea Angel, Bangladesh

Cdr:	MajGen Henry C. Stackpole III, USMC
DepCdr:	Col Edward G. Hoffman, USAF
CS:	Col Stephen E. Lindblom, USMC
SgtMaj:	SgtMaj Patrick W. McLane, USMC
J-1:	LtCol James R. Morris, USMC
J-2:	Cdr Joseph C. Levi, USN
J-3:	LtCol Gary W. Anderson, USMC
J-4A:	LtCol Christopher R. Mohr, USMC
J-6:	LtCol Dan P. Houston, USMC
Surgeon:	Capt John R. Downs MC, USNR
SJA:	Maj Manuel E. Supervielle, USA
PA:	LtCol James L. Vance, USMC

Joint Task Force Sea Angel (Forward), Chittagong

CS(Fwd):	Col Mike Ferguson, USAF
J-1(Fwd):	Maj D. C. Ward, USAF
J-2(Fwd):	LtCol Alan H. Dank, USMC
J-3(Fwd):	Capt Edward P. Anglim, USN
J-4:	Col Russell F. Bailes, Jr., USMC
J-6(Fwd):	Maj Charles E. Cooke, USMC

5th Marine Expeditionary Brigade

CG:	BGen Peter J. Rowe
CS:	Col Drake F. Trumpe
G-1:	Maj Leslie E. Garrett
G-2:	LtCol Malcolm Arnot
G-3:	LtCol Thorys J. Stensrud
G-4:	Col Eugene L. Gobeli
G-6:	LtCol William J. Cantu

Regimental Landing Team 5

CO:	Col Randolph A. Gangle
2d Bn, 5th Mar:	LtCol Kevin M. Kennedy
3d Bn, 5th Mar:	LtCol Donald R. Selvage
2d Bn, 11th Mar:	LtCol Paul A. Gido

Marine Aircraft Group 50

CO:	Col Randall L. West
HMLA-169:	LtCol Theron D. Rogers
HMH-772:	LtCol Thomas J. Miller
HMM-265:	LtCol John D. Holdstein

VMA-513:   Maj Eddie L. Holcomb
3d LAAD: Maj Gerald L. Troupe

Brigade Service Support Group 5
CO: Maj Robert G. Johnson

Appendix C
Task Organization

Command Element   **MajGen Henry C. Stackpole, III, USMC**

    Det III MEF
    Deployable JTF Augmentation Cell
    C-12 Det MCAS Iwakuni and MCAS Futenma
    4th Combat Communications Group (-)
        Contingency Operations Base 3
        Contingency Operations Base 5
    PAO Det
        PAO Det, MCB Camp S. D. Butler
        PAO Det, COMNAVFORJAPAN
        PAO Det, COMUSFOR, Subic Bay, RP
    Det 834th Air Logistics Division (ALD)
    Det 364th Civil Affairs Brigade
    Det 322d Civil Affairs Group
    Det 351st Civil Affairs Command

Marine Forces (MARFOR)

5th Marine Expeditionary Brigade   **BGen Peter J. Rowe, USMC**

    Command Element
        Headquarters Company
        5th SRISG
        Det 1st Radio Bn
        Det Company A, 9th Comm Bn
        Det 4th Force Recon Company
        Det 4th Military Police Company
        Det 31st ITT
        Det 14th CIT
        Det 4th SCAMP
    Ground Combat Element
        Regimental Landing Team 5
            Headquarters, 5th Marines
            TOW Platoon, HQ Company, 23d Marines
            2d Bn, 5th Marines
            3d Bn, 5th Marines
            3d Bn, 11th Marines
            Company B, 1st Reconnaissance Bn
            Company A (Rein), 4th Tank Bn
            Company A (Rein), 4th Assault Amphibian Bn
            Company A (Rein), 4th Light Armored Infantry Bn
            Company A, 4th Combat Engineer Bn
            Company B, 1st Combat Engineer Bn
            Company F, 2nd Bn, 25th Marines

    Aviation Combat Element

Marine Aircraft Group 50
    Det MASS-6
    Det MWSS-372
    HMM-265
    HMLA-169
    HMH-772, Det A
    VMA-513, Det B
    3d LAAD Bn
Combat Service Support Element
    Brigade Service Support Group 5
        Headquarters
        Det 1st Landing Support Bn
        Det 7th Motor Transport Bn
        Det 1st Medical Bn
        Det 1st Dental Bn
        Det 7th Engineer Support Bn
        Det 1st Supply Bn
        Det 1st Maintenance Bn
        Det 7th Communications Bn

Contingency Marine Air-Ground
Task Force 2-91   LtCol Larry A. Johnson, USMC

Navy Forces (NAVFOR)

Task Group 76.6	**RAdm Stephen S. Clarey, USN**
USS *Tarawa* (LHA 1)	Capt Wirt R. Fladd, USN
USS *Vancouver* (LPD 2)	Capt Clarence W. Burck, USN
USS *Juneau* (LPD 10)	Capt Tom A. Fitzgibbons, USN
USS *Mount Vernon* (LSD 39)	Cdr David E. Myers, USN
USS *Frederick* (LST 1184)	Cdr Thomas W. Thiesse, USN
USS *Barbour County* (LST 1195)	Cdr Joseph B. Wilkinson, USN
USS *Anchorage* (LSD 36)	Capt Terence P. Labrecque, USN
USS *St. Louis* (LKA 116)	Capt John W. Peterson, USN
Environmental and Preventive Medicine Unit-6	Cdr Kenneth R. Ockermann, MC, USN

Air Forces (AFFOR)   Col Edward G. Hoffman, USAF

Det 374th Tactical Airlift Wing
    21st Tactical Airlift Squadron (-)
    345th Tactical Airlift Squadron (-)
Det 603d Airlift Control Squadron
Det 8th Mobile Aerial Port Squadron (MAPS)

Army Forces (ARFOR)   **LtCol Thomas F. Elzey, USA**
     4-25 Aviation Battalion (-)
     Det 84th Engineer Battalion

Special Operations Forces (SOF)   **LtCol George W. Norwood, USAF**
     Joint Special Operations Task Force
          1st Battalion, 1st Special Forces Group (Airborne) (USA)
          17th Special Operations Squadron (USAF)
          Det 2, 1723d Special Tactics Squadron (USAF)

Appendix D
United States Assistance
Provided Cyclone Disaster Effort

OFDA Funding	Amount	Description
Grants to NGOs		
CARE	$2,326,850	24 Relief Centers
Save the Children (USA)	$280,739	9,000 families in urban Fund Chittagong and Sitakunda
The Asia Foundation	$366,000	24,200 families in urban Chittagong and Sitakunda
Pathfinder Fund	$294,000	7,000 families in urban Chittagong, Rawzan, and Fatikchari
World Vision	$250,000	Relief in urban Chittagong and Bandarban
International Center for Diarrheal Disease Control, Bangladesh	$75,000	Technical assistance to NGOs and BDG on water, sanitation, and diarrheal disease control
Helen Keller International	$91,000	Distress monitoring in affected areas
Other OFDA-Funded Assistance		
Ambassador's Fund	$25,000	Contributed to Prime Minister's Relief Fund
Disaster Relief Staff Support	$12,850	Personal Service Contractor
ORS Production/ Supply Assessment	$7,150	Consultant
4 Million Water Purification Tablets	$512,000	Distributed to seven NGOs
ORS sachets and inputs	$184,000	For local production and distribution of ORS

Infrastructure Damage Assessment (with World Bank)	$295,000	Assessment of damage to roads, bridges, schools, BDG clinics, and utilities
Local Support Costs	$15,000	
Additional NGO Grants	$390,411	
OFDA Total	**$5,125,000**	

Other USAID Funding

Water Purification Tablets	$14,000	Donated to BDG and NGOs
Up to 55,000 MT of Title II wheat	$11,000,000	Replenish stocks used for emergency feeding
Rehabilitate Rural Electricity Board equipment	$2,000,000	Reprogramming USAID Development Assistance funds

Department of Defense

Medical Supplies	$2,000,000	From pre-positioned stocks
Corps of Engineer Personnel	15 persons	Repair Chittagong Airport
Relief Commodities	$26,000,000	Delivered by C-5s, C-141s, and C-130s
Joint Task Force Sea Angel	$6,350,000	Helicopters, amphibious craft, personnel, water purification units, medical supplies, food, etc.

Non-OFDA Contributions	**$47,364,000**
Total Assistance	**$52,489,000**

Appendix E
Joint Meritorious Unit Award

Citation

to accompany the award of the

Joint Meritorious Unit Award

to the

Joint Task Force SEA ANGEL

Joint Task Force SEA ANGEL distinguished itself by exceptional meritorious service from 10 May 1991 to 13 June 1991. During this period, as one of the largest military disaster relief forces ever assembled, Joint Task Force SEA ANGEL established a record of accomplishments that also made it one of the most successful. In response to the Bangladesh Government's request for humanitarian disaster relief assistance, in the wake of a tropical cyclone and tidal surge that claimed in excess of 139,000 lives and left millions homeless, soldiers, sailors, airmen, and marines were notified and within hours deployed and rapidly formed into a cohesive, dedicated team. Displaying exceptional airmanship in all kinds of weather extremes, the Air Force component flew 194 missions moving 2,430 tons of relief materials. Concurrently, the Army's "Blackhawks" flew 805 sorties for distribution of 886 tons, while the Navy and Marine aviation assets from the 7th Fleet's Amphibious Ready Group flew 969 sorties, distributing 700 tons of food, medicine, and construction materials. Equally monumental was the surface lift effort of the Navy and Marine Team in the Bay of Bengal's treacherous currents and debris-filled, unmarked river channels, which resulted in remote areas receiving 1,487 tons of life-sustaining medicines and supplies and 266,000 gallons of potable water produced by the Reverse Osmosis Water Purification Crews. Simultaneously, 6 Medical Contact Teams provided a host of medical analyses, treated over 15,000 patients and orchestrated the distribution [of] 38 metric tons of medical supplies. As a result of these efforts, representatives of the United States Agency for International Development estimated that critical supplies and medicines reached in excess of one million people and likely saved from starvation and serious illness over 100,000 others. In addition, appraisals compiled by engineers and the Special Forces Disaster Assessment Teams will be invaluable to the future self-directed restoration and development of the Bangladesh coastal infrastructure. Furthermore, despite the hundreds of hours flown, the ever-changing weather extremes, the seaborne lift mission through some of the world's most treacherous waters, and thousand of individual efforts in every conceivable environment, Joint Task Force SEA ANGEL accomplished the mission without a single death, serious injury, accident, or incident. By their exemplary performance of duty, the members of Joint Task Force SEA ANGEL brought great credit upon themselves and to the Department of Defense.

Given under my hand this 15th day of January 1992

//Colin L. Powell
Chairman, Joint Chiefs of Staff

Index